NUTS

Edible

Series Editor: Andrew F. Smith

EDIBLE is a revolutionary series of books dedicated to food and drink that explores the rich history of cuisine. Each book reveals the global history and culture of one type of food or beverage.

Already published

Apple Erika Janik *Barbecue* Jonathan Deutsch and Megan J. Elias *Beef* Lorna Piatti-Farnell *Beer* Gavin D. Smith *Bread* William Rubel *Cake* Nicola Humble *Caviar* Nichola Fletcher *Champagne* Becky Sue Epstein *Cheese* Andrew Dalby *Chocolate* Sarah Moss and Alexander Badenoch *Cocktails* Joseph M. Carlin *Curry* Colleen Taylor Sen *Dates* Nawal Nasrallah *Eggs* Diane Toops *Game* Paula Young Lee *Gin* Lesley Jacobs Solmonson *Hamburger* Andrew F. Smith *Herbs* Gary Allen *Hot Dog* Bruce Kraig *Ice Cream* Laura B. Weiss *Lemon* Toby Sonneman *Lobster* Elisabeth Townsend *Milk* Hannah Velten *Mushroom* Cynthia D. Bertelsen *Offal* Nina Edwards *Olive* Fabrizia Lanza *Oranges* Clarissa Hyman *Pancake* Ken Albala *Pie* Janet Clarkson *Pineapple* Kaori O'Connor *Pizza* Carol Helstosky *Pork* Katharine M. Rogers *Potato* Andrew F. Smith *Rum* Richard Foss *Salmon* Nicolaas Mink *Sandwich* Bee Wilson *Soup* Janet Clarkson *Spices* Fred Czarra *Tea* Helen Saberi *Whiskey* Kevin R. Kosar *Wine* Marc Millon

Nuts

A Global History

Ken Albala

REAKTION BOOKS

Published by Reaktion Books Ltd
33 Great Sutton Street
London EC1V ODX, UK
www.reaktionbooks.co.uk

First published 2014

Printed and bound in China
by Toppan Printing Co. Ltd

A catalogue record for this book is available
from the British Library

ISBN 978 1 78023 282 9

Contents

Introduction

I realize that writing this book will forever label me a nutty professor. So be it. I love nuts, even though they are really rather odd. It is not the flavour that makes them so – in my mind this is the perfect combination of sweetness and aromatic oils, preferably roasted, with a hint of salt. Nor is it the texture, which is half the pleasure – that satisfying primal crunch which echoes through your skull cavity as you chomp down on nuts. I mean that the nuts themselves are strange. Many are certainly familiar, while others are almost completely unknown, but they all have their quirks. Moreover, we take nuts for granted without thinking much about them. My purpose in writing this is simply to get you to consider nuts more carefully: how they grow, where their names come from and what they mean to the people who use them. I want you to eat more nuts. I want to inspire you with their stories, which have been drawn from around the world and from different periods in history. Despite their peculiarities, they are all delicious in their own ways, and usually pretty good for you too.

Most people throughout history have valued nuts, which is unusual because the majority of foods have had their detractors at some point in time. Normally the meaning of an individual ingredient or recipe will change over time. What is rare and exotic in one period seems humdrum in another; what is expensive and a mark of distinction in one place is considered unpalatable elsewhere. What is used to promote health at one time is later taboo. Nuts defy these radical shifts in meaning over time and place. In fact, I think they may be one of the few foods whose social and cultural meanings have remained pretty much stable over time and in many different cultures.

There are few other foods that have remained in favour everywhere. The fashion for bread may rise and fall; the virtues of meat may be extolled by one generation and vilified in the next; wine has always had its champions and critics at each others' throats; forgotten fruits like pomegranates have enjoyed brief spots in the limelight. But nuts, everywhere you look, have been eaten happily and have usually been considered good for promoting health. This is especially the case today, but in the past few people advised against eating nuts altogether. They were never stigmatized as disgusting, never neglected or disdained by any culture. In fact, they have generally been considered quite elegant and sophisticated, if resolutely natural. Nuts do contain a lot of fat, but we're told it's good fat. Since they're usually minimally processed, they seem wholesome, unspoiled by the hands of humans and protected by their hard shells. It is true that more people are allergic to nuts nowadays than to most other foods, but this, so some say, is the result of all the processed food, antibiotics and pollution we ingest – and it does seem to be a modern phenomenon.

Nuts of course are not a staple. They did not change the course of world history, as did domesticated grains and the spice trade. However, it is their very humility that lends them grace and beauty. We don't need to eat nuts and they almost never form the centre of a meal. They're usually used as a snack, a garnish or something buried in a sweet bar, almost as an afterthought. They are most likely to show up before a meal in a little bowl, with cocktails. Nonetheless, it is hard not to love nuts. They are eminently charming, sophisticated and at the same time down to earth. They are also wonderfully varied in form and flavour. One could never mistake the seductive smoothness of a pine nut for the brazen sassiness of a Brazil nut. Pecans speak unmistakably of their origin. The tantalizing aroma of toasted almonds is like nothing else on Earth. I do hope that by the end of this little book you will have come to love nuts as much as I do. Let's get cracking!

Wizened chestnut trees painted by Camille Pissarro at Louveciennes in 1872.

I
What is a Nut?

Defining a nut botanically is not as simple as it sounds. It is technically a type of fruit with a hard shell. Linnaeus, the father of taxonomy, simply called it *semen tectum epidermide ossea* which means a seed with a hard, bony skin. But a nut is actually not a seed, like that found inside an apple or peach, which is why an almond is not a nut botanically. Neither are pine nuts or pistachios; all three are seeds. Peanuts are not nuts but legumes, and soy nuts, corn nuts and Grape Nuts are not nuts (the latter actually have nothing to do with either grapes or nuts). Surprisingly, the Brazil nut is a seed too; the coconut is a drupe, a kind of fruit in which the stone is derived from the ovary wall of the flower. Since Linnaeus's time there has been so much division and confusion over the term 'nut' that some modern botanists simply avoid using it altogether.[1]

Dispensing with the penumbra of botanical classification, here is my concise definition of a nut, following the dictates of common culinary usage: nuts (noun, plural) are things that grow on trees, have hard shells and are edible. All things commonly referred to as nuts are discussed here.

Nuts must be, proverbially, hard to crack. They must also be crunchy rather than soft and gelatinous, like the inside of a peach pit, which would otherwise be a nut, like the close relative of the peach, the almond. Apricot kernels sometimes do pass as nuts, however, especially in China, but also in amaretti biscuits, which people assume are flavoured with almonds. The seeds of other plants come strikingly close as well, those of the cheerful sunflower especially; as much as I would love to add them to the rank of noble tree-borne nuts, in gastronomic terms they remain lowly seeds. There are so many other things that simply can't be considered as culinary nuts, such as pumpkin seeds, tiger nuts (which are tubers) and lotus seeds.

Although there are hundreds of plant species that produce seeds which technically qualify as nuts, inedibility is grounds for immediate dismissal from coverage here. We must thus omit the horse chestnut, the beautiful buckeye and especially the nux vomica, from which strychnine is extracted. However, there are some poisonous nuts that we simply cannot avoid. Have you ever wondered why we never see cashews in the shell? The shell actually contains a powerful toxic irritant (the plant that produces cashews is in the poison ivy family). Bitter almonds are used in almond extract and pastries, though a few handfuls contain enough cyanide to kill a person.

Poisonous nuts aside, this book is not restricted to the common nuts like almonds, walnuts and pistachios, but includes some perfectly magnificent exotics, such as the mongongo of the San bushmen, and the areca, alias the betel nut, of Southeast Asia. There are many more nuts that deserve to be better known, plus a few that we often forget are nuts – like the nutmeg, despite its name, the cola nut and the coconut.

This book provides concise descriptions of the meaning of nuts throughout history and around the world; their uses in the kitchen and in maintaining health, and all the multifarious ways in which they have been processed into comestible goods, including oils, butters, nut-based milks and edible gums. As we shall see, nuts are eminently versatile and have been used in ways far beyond the out-of-hand snack that normally comes to mind. Because of their high fat content they serve as the base for high-calorie trail mixes and are excellent vegetarian fare as well, sometimes replicating dairy products perfectly: properly made fresh almond milk, for example, is a dead ringer for cow's milk.

Many nuts are attached to or within a fruit, the flesh of which we rarely see for sale, though this too can be edible. The green flesh surrounding the unripe walnut, for example, can be pickled or soaked in alcohol to make the Italian elixir known as nocino. Immature almonds can be eaten whole, green fruit, shell and all. Even green unripe pistachios can be eaten. Cashews, too, have a red edible fruit, or 'apple', which is very fragile and is normally made into jam or an astringent juice. The original pineapple, from which the Caribbean fruit gets its name in English, is the green nut-bearing pine cone. On the other hand some nuts – true nuts like the acorn – have

The cashew nut protrudes from the fruit like a sore thumb. Its shell is caustic.

Hazelnuts in their frilly green smocks.

an exposed fruitless shell. Others are even more peculiar: the hazelnut wears a frilly green smock.

Primitive Nuts

There are nuts that have been harvested as food for many millennia, and of course eaten by our animal relatives even longer, but they have resisted systematic cultivation. Some species, such as pecans, remained wild until fairly recently; Brazil nuts are still all harvested from the wild. This and their association with wild forests has given nuts a primitive appeal, as if these were the original foods of our ancient forebears before the advent of civilization. Nuts and berries are the original unprocessed foods, if you will; they are nature's food, appropriate for vegetarians and fruitarians like Adam and

Eve, because one can eat them without murdering a living organism. Like squirrels, we can store them for the winter, and they provide ample nutrition.

In many respects nuts have retained this wild association throughout history right to the present day, among health-food advocates, in raw-food diets and even among medical professionals who tout the benefits of nuts in preventing heart disease and other ailments. We seem to have a strong inner suspicion that these are the foods we evolved to eat, long before the introduction of cultivated grains and other farmed produce. 'Going wild' almost instantly conjures up a diet of nuts and berries.

Probably no other nut retains these associations as vividly as the acorn, which comes from trees of the genus *Quercus*. Unlike other nuts the majority of acorns require extensive processing to remove the bitter tannins within them, and this is done simply by pounding them and leaching them with water. The Native Americans of California subsisted on acorns, which explains why they had no need for agriculture.

Acorns

Acorns have been eaten by humans for millennia – mostly by those living in mountain wilds or by people who appreciated the oak's remarkable fecundity and had no reason to plant grain crops, such as Native Americans. Europeans ate them too in prehistoric times and even after. The ancients imagined them to be among the first foods of humans, in the Golden Age, when humans lived in a simple vegetarian, peaceful paradise, freely gathering sweet acorns without true labour. The idyllic Arcadia was said to be inhabited by *balanaphagoi* – eaters of acorns – and no other food so vividly conjures up images of primitive simplicity. Real people of course ate them during famines, but they still seemed to be a pure and wholesome food. The ancient Greek poet Hesiod says of just and peaceful people that

> The earth bears them victual in plenty, and on the mountains the oak bears acorns upon the top and bees in the midst. Their woolly sheep are laden with fleeces; their women bear children like their parents. They flourish continually with good things, and do not travel on ships, for the grain-giving earth bears them fruit.

The great Roman physician Galen tells a story of a famine during which country people ate the pigs that would normally have been kept fed on mast throughout the winter, then survived on the mast themselves for the rest of the winter. They boiled the acorns, baked them in hot ashes, and even

Dried California acorns after being shelled, before grinding, leaching and cooking.

Acorns are a true botanical nut, though they are rarely eaten anymore by humans.

made a soup with honey and milk. There is no suggestion that this constituted privation or hardship. Galen insists that acorns are just as nutritious as grains, and long ago the Arcadians subsisted on them.[2]

Jean La Bruyère-Champier, the sixteenth-century food encyclopaedist, contends that before riotous luxury held sway men lived in caves, and that above all else which the Earth spontaneously bore as food, 'humans especially ate from acorn bearing trees', which furnished plentiful nourishment. In the pre-modern imagination acorns were the staple of the first palaeo diet.[3]

The commercial sale of acorns and even acorn flour is practically non-existent, and the few home producers who supply these online charge a hefty sum. If you really want to go wild, harvest acorns yourself. Make sure there are no little holes, which indicate that bugs live inside. White oak is the preferred species in the u.s. and in Europe it is the holm oak

(*Quercus ilex*), and sometimes you can find trees that bear nuts which you can eat right off the tree, or just after a quick roasting in their shells. Most will need to be dried thoroughly in a warm oven, or in a dry place for up to a year. When they have dried, crack open and discard the shells, and pound the acorns in a big mortar or grinding rock until they are fine and floury. A blender or food processor can also be used for this purpose. Put the flour in a cloth bag, place this in a large bowl or bucket, and let water flow over the flour gently, pouring over the sides so that it is washed gradually. Continue until the flour is sweet. Put the flour on a baking sheet and let it dry thoroughly in the oven, set at 50°C (120°F) or so.

Use the acorn flour as you would any non-glutinous flour, for pancakes, muffins and even cakes. A little mixed with bread flour will give risen bread a rich, nutty flavour. The proper way to cook acorn flour for the primitivist would be to heat up some volcanic rocks in a fire, then dump them in a tightly woven basket containing the acorn flour and water. This is then stirred until a smooth porridge is achieved, the rocks are removed and the porridge is eaten. My personal favourite, however, is the acorn crêpe – the instructions for making it are in the recipe section.

Brazil Nuts

Half a world away from the acorn, tropical Brazil nuts are the nuts of romance – not the elegant sophisticated kind of romance, but wild jungle love, deep in the heart of the Amazon. The Brazil nut is not a nut but a seed that grows in two rows like orange segments inside a heavy, round pod, in form and function not unlike a cannon ball, as those who have been struck by one plummeting hundreds of feet onto their heads can readily attest. Brazil nuts come not only from Brazil itself, but from across the tropical Amazon Basin, where they are collected by native peoples. This, no doubt, is the reason for the primitive association, but it may perhaps also be because despite the best efforts, Brazil nuts are not a cultivated food. There are few other plants that are commercially harvested from the wild on such a scale. The wild state of the massive trees (*Bertholletia excelsa*) that bear the nuts is due to the curious mode of propagation. This can only be performed by a special orchid bee that bears a prodigious tongue with which to probe the curvaceous depths of the flowers and pollinate them. The pod containing the nuts is so hard that it must be smashed with an axe, and the nuts likewise resist the most powerful nutcrackers, their odd three-sided shape making them particularly cumbersome to crack.

The unique shape of Brazil nuts allows them to fit snugly together like segments in a large pod.

Brazil nuts are mentioned by the Spanish in Peru as early as 1569, when Juan Álvarez de Maldonado, conqueror of the Amazon, commandeered a large supply to feed his soldiers. However, they did not become an article of commerce until centuries later. If you wanted Brazil nuts you simply had to go and get them, until the nineteenth century, when a few roads and boats plying the river made trade possible.

Perhaps the most remarkable thing about Brazil nuts is that due to their unique shape, when shelled and placed in a tin among their cousins, a principle of physics takes place: the Brazil nut effect, or granular convection. Have you ever noticed how the biggest nuts rise to the top of a tin of mixed nuts? You would expect them to sink to the bottom. There is a variety of explanations for the phenomenon but I think it's because people really want to pick them out first and so the Brazil nuts, longing to be eaten, nudge their way to the top of the can, pushing the lesser nuts down to the bottom. Woe betide the unfortunate latecomer left only with greasy little Spanish peanuts.

Coconuts

Another, though very different, tropical nut is the coconut. There cannot be a desert island without coconut palms (*Cocos nucifera*), bent over lazily while the waves lap the sandy shore. The coconut is remarkably versatile, too. Think of the cartoon character Yosemite Sam marooned on his tiny island fixing to eat his meal: 'tossed coconut salad, fresh coconut milk, New England boiled coconut . . . 20 years of coconut, I can't stand coconuts!' However, note that he did manage to live on coconuts for many years, which only points to the amazing amount of nutrition they provide.

Fresh coconuts with the husk, which is made into coir fibre, a word that derives from the Tamil *kayaru*.

Coconut shells tapped together to make a clopping noise were famously used as horse substitutes by the knights of King Arthur in the film *Monty Python and the Holy Grail*:

GUARD NO. 1: Where'd you get the coconuts?

ARTHUR: We found them.

GUARD NO. 1: Found them? In Mercia? The coconut's tropical!

ARTHUR: What do you mean?

GUARD NO. 1: Well, this is a temperate zone.

ARTHUR: The swallow may fly south with the sun or the house martin or the plover may seek warmer climes in winter, yet these are not strangers to our land.

GUARD NO. 1: Are you suggesting that coconuts migrate?

Fittingly, in Sanskrit coconuts are called *kalpavriksha*, or tree that provides all the necessities of life. The fibre around a coconut, called coir, is used for mats and ropes. The shell makes a magnificent cup – fine examples go back to the Middle Ages, when coconut cups were rare and exotic. Sap from the coconut palm can be tapped and cooked down into sugar, fermented into palm wine and palm vinegar, and even distilled into fiery arrak. There are not many other nut trees from which you can make hooch.

Coconut water is sweet and pleasant, and has suddenly become popular among the health conscious. It can be purchased bottled or in ecofriendly boxes for not inconsiderable sums of money, to restore electrolytes. It should not be confused with coconut milk, which is made by grating or scraping coconut flesh, then soaking and straining it. Coconut milk is among the most delicious ingredients on Earth, but unless you are really proficient and have a lot of time, it's best to buy it in a can. Simmered with kaffir lime leaves, chillies, some fresh turmeric root and galangal, it is the ideal base for just about anything else you would like to throw in – the very heart of Southeast Asian cuisine. Speaking of heart, the so-called heart of the palm – the tree is actually killed if it is removed – is a tender, crunchy white stick of sweet vegetable. In a tin it leaves much to be desired, but fresh it is a revelation.

Then there's coconut oil, once reviled by health fanatics because saturated at room temperature, but now miraculously revived as a natural food, labelled virgin coconut oil. It is spectacular as a cooking medium and the flavour is unmistakable in a stir-fry and even in sweets, as long as you're using raw, pressed coconut oil and not the industrial 'refined, bleached and deodorized' variety. It is pressed from either fresh coconuts or *copra*, dried coconut flesh. The oil also has many industrial uses, in soaps and lotions, and even in paint and as a fuel.

The coconut flesh itself is a most versatile ingredient. It goes equally well with savoury and sweet recipes. The latter include macaroons, coconut cream pie and tooth-achingly

Nuts sold
in a shop in
Rishikesh, India.

sugary Indian coconut barfi and coconut flan. The unmistakable chocolate-covered shredded, sweetened coconut
confection is called Mounds, or when topped with whole
almonds, Almond Joy. Savoury dishes include coconut-crusted
shrimp. One of the best drinks ever invented is the 'No Problem' cocktail of Jamaica, which contains coconut, pineapple,
lime and rum.

Just the smell of coconut can evoke puffy red sunbathers
basking on a beach (in the u.s. state of New Jersey, for example,
the custom is to rub coconut oil on human bodies before frying them in the sun). Even more oddly, chunks of coconut are

sold on the streets in Paris, France, kept moist by a fine mist of continuously sprayed water. The weirdest thing about coconuts is their origin. They are commonly thought to originate in the Indian Ocean, but ancient fossils of close relatives are found in South America. Can they have made the trans-Pacific journey on their own, floating on the waves, as it were, and truly migratory? Maybe they were carried by Polynesian people all the way to the Americas? There were coconuts on the west coast of Panama when the Spanish first landed there in the sixteenth century, though no one there seems to have wanted to eat them.

Then think of the form of the coconut. Scraggly and hairy, with a monkey face at one end. That, supposedly, is where the name comes from; *coco* in Spanish means monkey face.

The Shapes of Nuts

The shapes of nuts appear to have been of particular fascination to our forebears – especially when it came to the things that nuts reminded them of. The use of the term nuts in reference to testicles dates back only to the 1860s. Before then it more commonly referred to what we now call the head, or glans, which actually means acorn in Latin. The word gland in English derives from *glandula* – a little acorn. In 1565 Thomas Cooper's *Thesaurus* described the glans as 'the nutte of a man's yarde'.

Normally, however, the nut referred to an actual human head. The resemblance of the walnut to the human brain, with its two convoluted hemispheres, is unmistakable. According to the doctrine of signatures espoused by Paracelsian alchemists, earthly matter is assigned shape and colour as a means by which God reveals its inner virtues and use in medicine. Thus red substances are good for the blood, heart-shaped plants for the heart and logically walnuts for the head. According to William Coles's *Adam in Eden*:

> Wall-nuts have the perfect Signature of the Head: The outer husk or green Covering, represent the Pericranium, or outward skin of the skull, whereon the hair groweth, and therefore salt made of those husks or barks, are exceeding good for wounds in the head. The inner wooddy shell hath the Signature of the Skull, and the little yellow skin, or Peel, that covereth the Kernell of the hard Meninga and Pia-mater, which are the thin scarfes that envelope the brain. The Kernel hath the very figure of the Brain, and therefore it is very profitable for the Brain, and resists poysons; For if the Kernel be bruised, and moystned with the quintessence of Wine, and laid upon the Crown of the Head, it comforts the brain and head mightily.[4]

The shape of an almond suggested something altogether different. The mandorla, an upright almond, was a religious symbol throughout the ancient world. The intersection of two circles, the geometric ratio of the almond shape, or mandorla, was believed by the Pythagoreans to be a key to understanding the harmony of the universe. Moreover, it was considered to be a symbol of the intersection of the earthly and divine planes of existence. This was taken up by early Christians as a symbol of creation, not coincidentally resembling the outline of the birth passage in our species. When Jesus was depicted within the mandorla shape, it was a reminder that he bridges the two worlds and though born of a woman, is nonetheless equally divine. On its side the almond shape more closely resembles a fish, which was used by early

Christians as a secret symbol to recognize each other and worship together. This was later explained with the acrostic ΙΧΘΥΣ (Ichthys), meaning in Greek: *Iesous Christos, Theou Huios, Soter* (Jesus Christ, God's Son, Saviour). The mandorla shape, depicting Jesus, Mary and saints, continued to be a popular motif right up to the Renaissance.

Then there is the coco de mer (*Lodoicea maldivica*), which grows only in the Seychelles – a group of tiny remote islands north of Madagascar. Imagine something like a double coconut, but in size and form exactly like a female groin, that is with a belly, two legs and sometimes a furry patch and a pair of buttocks on the reverse side. These nuts are sometimes also called love nuts. They are actually the world's largest seeds, weighing as much as 92 pounds. The name *maldivica* comes from the Maldives, where the nuts were washed ashore long before the Seychelles were discovered by humans. An earlier species name was *callipyge*, which means beautiful rump in Greek. Early European explorers naturally saved the choicest specimens for their private collections.

The alluring
and suggestive
coco de mer.

Jackfruit hanging from a tree.

One of the weirdest of nuts is found within one of the weirdest of fruits – the jackfruit (*Artocarpus heterophyllus*), a huge, swollen tumescence growing off the side of the trunk of a tropical tree. The fruit can weigh as much as 45 kg (100 lb) and has a peculiar nubbin-patterned skin. Inside the sweet pulp are hundreds of starchy nuts that can be boiled or roasted.

The nut with the weirdest shape of all is the water caltrop, or ling nut (of the genus *Trapa*). This is found across Asia

Fearsome water caltrops look like the spikes used to stop horses in medieval warfare.

and Europe, and in flavour is something like a water chestnut. Its shape is perfectly demonical. The name comes from the caltrop, derived from the Latin *calcitrapa* (foot trap). Children should be familiar with the shape, which is similar to that of the jacks used in a game of the same name. Jacks are little spikes which you swoop up in between bounces of a rubber ball. Originally these were sharp and scattered on fields to impede charging horses in battle. There are even modern versions that puncture car tyres. In any case, the fruit sometimes looks exactly like a spiked jack, especially in European species. Elsewhere it looks more like a monster with horns, which explains why the nuts are also called devil pods. In China they are called buffalo head fruit, and some do look exactly like that. They were once sold on European streets roasted, much like chestnuts, but now appear to be nearly extinct in Europe. They are still cultivated in China and India, where they are eaten boiled or even made into flour.

Nuts in Human Health

Above all foods, nuts have had powerful medicinal associations since ancient times. Perhaps this was because of their distinctly astringent taste on the tongue, or their palpable oil content. Usually classified as heating and drying, they were commonly used in corrective regimens and as more powerful drugs for a wide variety of conditions. They were also considered dangerous for people already prone to bilious conditions. Take, for example, this detailed description by the great botanist Pedanius Dioscorides (*c.* AD 40–90), a man who travelled the ancient world in search of new medicinal plants. He wrote:

> Walnuts, which some call Persian are difficult to digest, harmful to the stomach, bilious, cause headaches, are of no use for those with a cough, and are useful for a vomit if eaten when fasting. When eaten with rue and figs, and at the end of a meal or before, they counteract poison. If eaten in great quantity they expel worms. They also help inflammation of the breasts, abscesses and dislocations with some honey and rue. And with onions, salt and honey, they are good for those bitten by dogs or men. When burnt with the calyx and applied to the navel they assuage colic. The shell if burned, ground with wine and oil on the head of infants nourishes the hair and fills up bald spots. But the nut when burned finely ground and applied with wine, stops menstruation. The kernels of old nuts, if chewed and laid on as a plaster, cures gangrene, carbuncles, stye in the eye, and hair loss, is an immediate remedy. Oil is pressed out of them also. Fresher ones are sweeter, less harmful to the stomach, they are mixed with garlic to take away the bitterness, and they remove bruises on the body.[5]

There was comparable medical interest in almonds. 'Almonds are burning but nutritious; burning because they are oily, and nutritious because they are fleshy', according to Hippocrates. The passage suggests that the oil in almonds makes them qualitatively hot, according to the principles of humoral medicine, which would serve to scour out the body's passages, and the statement that they are fleshy seems to suggest that they are solid and substantial. Diocles is no less succinct:

> Almonds . . . are nourishing and good for the bowels, and are moreover, calorific because they contain some of the properties of millet. The green are less unwholesome than the dry, the soaked than the unsoaked, the roasted than the raw.

Apart from recognizing various types of almond, it is clear that the early medical writers were a little ambivalent about this nut's effect on the body. At the very least, they seem to have recognized that almonds were heating. Diphilus of Siphnos, writing shortly after Diocles, claimed that:

> Almonds are diuretic, attenuating, cathartic, and of little nutrition. Dried almonds, however, are much more windy and apt to lie on the stomach than the green, which to be sure, have a poor flavour and are less nourishing. But if they are blanched when still tender though full grown, they are milky and of better flavour.

It appears that he may have been speaking of bitter almonds in the first line and sweet almonds in various stages of ripeness in the latter.

The most important medical authority of the ancient world was Galen of Pergamum, physician to the Emperor

The stately English or Persian walnut beside two smaller and harder New World species.

Marcus Aurelius and subsequent Roman rulers. In his book on the properties of food Galen writes:

> These nuts do not possess much by way of astringency. A cleansing and attenuating quality is prevalent in them, by means of which they purge the inwards and act toward the expectoration of moist matter from the lungs and chest. Some of them have such an overriding power of cutting through thick and viscous moisture that they cannot be eaten because of their bitterness.[6]

Clearly these medicinal qualities refer to bitter almonds. He also states, like Hippocrates, that they have a fatty and oily quality, but afford little nourishment to the body, which contrasts directly with earlier sources.

Roman authors also mentioned almonds, and gave different opinions on them. Pliny, for example, gives many more medical uses for bitter almonds: they provoke sleep and sharpen the appetite, and act as a diuretic and emmenagogue. They are also useful against headache and fever. Presumably their purging qualities were thought to drive out the fever, rather than counteract or cool it. Of sweet almonds Pliny only says: 'their remedial properties are not so extensive; still however, they are of a purgative nature, and are diuretic. Eaten fresh they are difficult of digestion.'

In modern times we seem to suffer from the same ambivalence. In some periods of history the advice was to avoid nuts because of their high fat content, but today they are considered among the ideal foods from a health perspective. Walnuts are rich in omega-3 fatty acids and increase the good kind of HDL cholesterol and lower the bad kind (LDL). Almonds contain a great deal of vitamin A, which is an antioxidant and may prevent Alzheimer's. Pistachios are full of lutein, which is good for the eyes. Hazelnuts contain folate, a B vitamin, and other B vitamins that are good for the heart and may help prevent cancer. Pecans are also powerful antioxidants. Nut oils are peddled today exactly like snake oil would have been a century ago, as a remedy for nearly any ailment. Obviously the theories have changed and no doubt will again in the future. Nevertheless, throughout history physicians have always seemed to find medicinal properties in nuts.

2

Nuts to Chew

There are certain nuts that, while not exactly eaten, are chewed as a stimulant, breath freshener and general social palliative. The two most important nuts for chewing are the areca, which is used throughout Southeast Asia, and the cola nut, which is prevalent in West Africa. There is undoubtedly something soothing in the mere process of chewing; it promotes contemplation, and it seems as though we have been hardwired since prehistoric times to enjoy gnawing away on things like tough bark, or especially gum. How pleasant, then, that chewing can also offer a bit of a buzz, as these two nuts do.

The areca, or betel nut, which grows on a palm tree (genus *Areca*), is not chewed on its own. It is usually sliced and wrapped in a betel pepper leaf, folded up in a little package – called a betal quid – along with spices like cardamom, cloves and even tobacco. In India this is called *paan*. A touch of lime paste – calcium carbonate – catalyses the vital alkaloids to induce a state of euphoria. *Catechu*, or *cutch*, a dark tannic extract of an acacia species, is also sometimes added to the package. The dry hard nuts themselves can be purchased in a good Indian food shop; and from experience I can tell you that they taste of nothing and have no effect at all. You really need all the other ingredients, and the leaves, which have to be fresh. I had

Areca nuts grow on a kind of palm tree.

the opportunity to taste a betel quid once in Oxford when a friend brought some from India. Whether the nut or the company induced euphoria, I cannot say. In habitual users the teeth become completely red.

The betel quid has its aficionados as well as its detractors. It is usually chewed after dinner, by both men and women, throughout India, Cambodia, Thailand, Laos and Vietnam, all the way to the Philippines and Indonesia, and through the South Pacific. The word areca comes from the Malay word *adakka*, and the nut is native to Malaysia as well. In Vietnam betal quids are used in wedding ceremonies because just as the areca nut and betel leaf are considered to be inseparable, so too should the husband and wife be. The fresh leaves and nuts are sold in markets where large communities of Vietnamese and Cambodians reside in the U.S., though there they are prominently labelled 'For Ceremonial Purposes Only, Not For Human Consumption'. Officially the nut is classified as carcinogenic. Then there's the problem of spitting – it stains pavements red and gives the lurid impression that someone has just been gushing blood.

On the other hand, chewing *paan* is a practice of venerable antiquity. The ancient Sanskrit *Sushruta Samhita*, an Ayurvedic medical text, says:

> A betel-leaf prepared with cloves, camphor, nutmeg, lime, araca-nut . . . should be taken (chewed after meals) as it tends to cleanse the mouth, impart a sweet aroma to it, enhance its beauty and cleanse and strengthen the voice, the tongue, the teeth, the jaws and the sense organs.

Betel (bertel) box, early 19th century.

An areca nut vendor on the island of Hainan, China.

It also soothes the body and prevents throat disease. Moreover, betel serves as Vájikarana, or one of the things that promote sexual arousal, for which the treatise recommends

> Various kinds of (nutritious and palatable) food and (sweet, luscious and refreshing) liquid cordials, speech that gladdens the ears, and touch which seems delicious to the skin, clear nights mellowed by the beams of the full moon and damsels young, beautiful and gay, dulcet songs that charm the soul and captivate the mind, use of betel leaves, wine and (sweet scented) flowers.[1]

The kola nut, fruit of the kola tree (genus *Cola*) is another chewed stimulant, native to tropical West Africa. The flavouring, or at least the artificial simulacrum of it nowadays, will be familiar as a soft drink, but when the nut is sliced and chewed its flavour is said to be very bitter, gradually becoming sweet. It contains a good dose of caffeine, so is particularly useful for staying awake or staving off hunger during a fast. Muslims who do not use alcohol are particularly happy to be offered a slice, which is considered a polite way to welcome guests. It is also offered to chieftains on special occasions, and in Nigeria is even used as an offering for the ancestral spirits. Ifà, the Yoruba divination system, uses kola to appease the orisha Orunmila, an ancestral spirit. The Hausa apparently eat so much of it that their teeth are stained red.

Like betel, kola is also featured in weddings, where it is shared by the bride and groom and their families. Kola thus symbolizes both sharing and the ability to come together and work out differences, and a kola nut is hung in the young couple's abode to remind them of this. The theme of working out differences also serves to remind the hundreds of different ethnic groups in Nigeria of unity, and the kola nut was even considered for the newly independent Nigeria's coat of arms with the motto 'unity and faith'. The current black shield, behind the wavy 'Y' representing rivers, could actually pass for a kola nut.

There's a scene in Chinua Achebe's classic novel *Things Fall Apart* in which a one of the characters affirms that 'He who brings kola, brings life.' The phrase appears similar to one used to advertise a popular soft drink: 'Coke adds life.' However, the cola nut must be fresh. If you order some online, presumably to make homemade cola, it will come crushed into little pieces and taste of absolutely nothing. It's much better to find some fresh nuts and share them with someone.

Among the chewing nuts you probably wouldn't expect nutmeg (*Myristica fragrans*), but actually it is relatively close in form to the other nuts described above. You can eat nutmeg, too, for its hallucinogenic properties, though this is hardly recommended as the active chemical, *myristicin*, makes you very sick. However, if you add a fine grating of a whole nutmeg to a soup or stew, to polenta, mashed potatoes or a pancake,

Few people realize that cola flavouring comes from an African nut.

or to top an eggnog, you will find that there are few spices so perfectly alluring.

Nutmeg was also important in world history. One of the conditions of the handover of New Amsterdam by the Dutch to the English was giving up the tiny island of Run in the Moluccas of Indonesia, which the Dutch wanted so that they could maintain their strict monopoly of the spice.

Unlike most other spices, nutmeg was not entirely banished from savoury dishes with the advent of modern cuisine. In fact, a hint of it goes well with almost anything as long as it isn't pre-ground and stale.

If you can, find the whole fruit – most of it nowadays comes from Grenada in the Caribbean. The great Dutch sixteenth-century botanist Rembert Dodoens likened the fruit to a walnut, which makes perfect sense.

> First it hath in the outside a greene thicke husk or shale, like to the outer shale of our walnut, wherewithall it is covered all over, under the same there is found certain thin skins like to cawles or nets, of a red or yellowish color, all jagged or pounced, of a verie pleasant savor.[2]

This is the aril, or mace, which has a distinct flavour all its own. Beneath this is the shell, and inside, the woody nutmeg. Like other culinary nuts it is full of oil, which is an aromatic flavouring that goes into cosmetics, processed foods and – of all things – Coca-cola.

The word nutmeg itself seems to come from the Italian *noce moscata*, the musky nut, which indeed it is. The genus name

Nutmeg fruits with the lacy red mace inside, surrounding the hard nutmeg.

Myristica in Latin, from the Greek μυριστικός, *myristikos* or 'balm', 'ointment', sounds even more exotic. How the state of Connecticut in the USA came to be known as the nutmeg state is a mystery. Some say it is because its inhabitants were so shrewd that they could sell you a wooden nutmeg. I suspect it has more to do with the New England spice trade, or perhaps the nutmeg's use in cooking, a subject to which we will turn presently.

3
Nuts in Cooking

Nuts may have featured in hominid meals long before we became fully human. The question is when they were first cooked and how. It is unlikely that cooked nuts featured in the meals of early man, unlike meat and tough vegetables and tubers that require cooking to be palatable. Without sophisticated tools, nuts are nearly impossible to cook. It would take great ingenuity to skewer them on a wooden stake to roast. Boiling in a pot doesn't do much for most nuts, though it's not unthinkable. Nuts baked in an earth oven might work nicely, alongside some slowly braised meat or vegetables, but there simply isn't much archaeological evidence for nut consumption in early man apart from nut shells.

Ancient Mesopotamian records dating back to 1600 BC, recipes written on clay tablets, include nuts like pistachios.[1] There is much debate about how nuts might have been served in the ancient Middle East, but I suspect that it might be as I ate them on a trip I once took to Australia, when, at the start of a meal my hosts presented a bowl of pounded, toasted almonds and spices into which we were invited to dip bread, first in olive oil then in a mixture called *dukkah*. The dish was unbelievably delicious. It hails from Syria, whence immigrants brought it to Australia. It's also popular in Egypt, where it is usually spelled *duqqa*, which in Arabic means to pound. The ingredients are wildly variable and can include coriander, cumin, cinnamon and pepper. You can use hazelnuts or pistachios as a substitute for the almonds. They should be crushed finely – not to a paste, but rather to a coarse powder.

Fascinatingly, a similar term is used among Yemenite Jews (*doukeh*) referring to *charoset*, the fruit and nut paste ceremonially eaten on Passover. It is basically the same as *dukkah*, but with the further addition of ground dates and raisins. The connection is not merely semantic. *Charoset* is a condiment that is mud-like in texture, and is seemingly descended directly from the Graeco-Roman world. It is made from ground nuts, fruits, spices, honey and vinegar or wine, into which one dips the bitter herbs (*maror*) or commonly matzoh. The great Roman cookbook attributed to Apicius has something much like this, a *Ypotrima* (meaning something ground up), with pepper, lovage, mint, pine nuts, raisins, dates, cheese, honey, vinegar, garum, oil and sweet wine.[2] The ceremony of Passover in general reflects aristocratic Graeco-Roman dining more than anything

Undyed pistachios in their shells, showing the green colour of the nut.

Charoset, a fruit and nut paste, on a ceremonial Seder plate for Passover. For recipe, see p. 111.

else (it includes reclining and drinking four glasses of wine), so the similarity here is probably not just coincidental. Recipes for *dukkah* and *charoset* can be found in the recipe section.

Chestnuts

The *Castanea sativa* tree produces edible chestnuts that are rather unlike any other nut, mostly because they are starchy and soft when cooked, rather than crunchy and oily. In this respect they are more like grains than nuts, and they have traditionally been eaten as a staple in many places, such as the Cevennes mountain range in the south of France and the Apennines in Italy. Being starchy, they readily lend themselves to cooking far above most other nuts. We think of 'chestnuts roasting on an open fire', which may be the best way to cook them, in a perforated pan of course so that they get nice and smoky, or broiled briefly in the oven. They should not be baked for too long – over-cooking makes them hard and inedible. They are also good boiled and unadorned, but sweetening them makes them infinitely more interesting.

Marrons glacés, which are candied chestnuts, are among the most delightful of confections, with a long historical pedigree. The first recorded recipe for them is in a book often attributed to the great seventeenth-century French chef François Pierre La Varenne, entitled *The French Confectioner*, though actually his name appears nowhere in any edition. Whether he penned the recipe is unimportant, but the procedure is: first you make a glaze with powdered sugar and orange-blossom water mixed together. Then roast some chestnuts on hot coals and remove the shells. Press the chestnuts gently to flatten them (without crushing them), glaze them on one side and cook in the upper part of an oven, then turn them over and glaze on the other side and cook in the same way.[3] The glaze will become hard when it dries, like on a glazed biscuit.

A man selling roasted chestnuts on the street.

There are also products made from *marrons glacés*. *Crème de marrons de l'Ardèche* is a sweetened purée that is used in desserts. When mixed with cream and topped with whipped cream, it supposedly looks like Mont Blanc, which is what this dessert is called. There were similar desserts in the Renaissance, for example a chestnut tart in Martino of Como's *Libro de Arte Coquinaria* (The Art of Cooking) written in the fifteenth century, which is made with boiled chestnuts, crushed and mixed with milk, passed through a sieve with fresh cheese, spices, sugar and eggs, and coloured yellow with saffron. In flavour and consistency the tart is remarkably like a pumpkin cheese-cake.[4] The original also includes pork belly, which makes it more interesting, though less familiar.

Harvesting chestnuts with a pole was a popular 19th-century pastime.

You can dry chestnuts, too, then grind them into a fine flour. Chestnut flour can alternatively be purchased in any good Italian shop or online, and is also made in Korea. Practically no other nut can be used this way in cooking, to make pancakes and crêpes, and the sublime castagnaccio, a chestnut flour cake. Sixteenth-century author Ortensio Lando credits the invention of the castagnaccio to a man from Lucca named Pillade.[5] It could equally have been invented in Liguria or anywhere in northern Italy, where it is appreciated. It is usually thin, but sometimes thick, and may contain raisins and pine nuts. Rosemary or fennel may be used in it, and it usually contains olive oil but not sugar, so it really isn't sweet. Just imagine a very dark, thin, dense cake, redolent of chestnuts. It is cooked in a very hot oven, so the surface beomes crispy

Vincent Van Gogh's *Chestnut Tree in Blossom*, painted in 1890 in Auvers-sur-Oise shortly before his death.

and cracked, while the interior stays moist. Some people serve it with ricotta or a drizzle of honey, both of which are very good.

Chestnut flour can also be used to make a variety of gnocchi. For this purpose, the chestnut flour (or a mixture of chestnut and potato flours) is simply combined with eggs and water, and the mixture is rolled into long coils, cut into little nubbins and dropped into boiling broth. The cooked gnocchi should be liberally sprinkled with grated hard cheese, or better yet served with a sauce made from Fontina or Robiola cheese, or a good Tomme. A classic bechamel sauce can be made with butter and a touch of flour cooked together, then mixed with scalded milk. Into that add grated cheese and stir, adding milk if you need to. Sautéed mushrooms make a good addition to the sauce. Pour the sauce over the gnocchi and serve immediately.

There are chestnuts elsewhere in the world apart from Europe. The Chinese have many chestnut species, and the majestic American chestnut (*Castanea dentata*) once covered most of the eastern mountain ranges until it was devastated by chestnut blight, a fungal disease.

Ginkgo

Ginkgo nuts come from what is without doubt the most beautiful of trees: *Ginkgo biloba*, with fan-shaped yellow leaves in autumn. It is native to China and is often called a living fossil because it has remained relatively unchanged for the last 270 million years, since the Jurassic period. The fruits are nasty, malodorous and caustic. However, within the odious fruits are nuts of astounding beauty and flavour. The fruits must be peeled and discarded wearing sturdy rubber gloves, preferably outdoors, and thrown away. The nuts are roasted and the thin shell is peeled off. They are used primarily in East Asian cookery, thrown into rice porridge or a stir-fry for crunch and depth of flavour, or skewered onto Japanese *yakitori*.

In the West, *G. biloba* is known for its reputed medicinal qualities. It supposedly aids the memory and has long been

Whole fruits from the gingko tree; the nuts are inside.

Shiny sweet orbs, the sweet interior of the ginkgo fruit.

suspected to be valuable in slowing the onset of Alzheimer's disease. In Chinese medicine its uses are far more varied and ancient. In China it was originally called *ya-chio*, or duck's foot, which it resembles. It is often claimed that gingko trees are planted on Buddhist temple grounds as objects of reverence, and they are mentioned as far back as the Song Dynasty. It may have been merely the age of the trees – some are reputedly a thousand years old – that led to this respect, rather than some special connection to Buddhism. More likely the nuts were commonly featured in vegetarian recipes, so were planted near temples for easy access. At weddings they are served with the shells dyed red for good luck.

Hazelnuts

The hazelnut takes the prize as the prettiest, if most dissembling of all nuts. Obviously it is trying to hide something, covered as it is by a lacy green kerchief. To further disguise its identity, it goes by many different names. The Latin genus name *Corylus* comes from the Greek *korys* – meaning a hood. Even in English the word hazel comes from the Anglo-Saxon *haesel*, meaning bonnet. The Greeks called hazelnuts Pontic nuts, since they came from Pontus on the north coast of what is today Turkey along the Black Sea – where most of them are still grown. The Romans, however, preferred to call them *avellanae*, meaning from Avella in southern Italy, where they are also still grown. It was apparently via sixteenth-century botanist Leonhart Fuchs that Linnaeus chose the name *avellana* for the species.[6] Don't be confused by the name filbert – it's really the same nut, named for the venerable seventh-century Filbert, alias St Philibert, on whose day (20 August) the nuts are said to be ready for harvesting, at least in Britain. However, how the people of Oregon, in the U.S., came to call these nuts filberts is a bit of a mystery.

The National Clonal Germplasm Respository in Corvallis, Oregon, is the best place to find out about hazelnuts. It is essentially a gene bank with cryogenically frozen nut tissues, just in case a pathogen damages the hazelnut crop. This is a multimillion-dollar industry in these parts, and if a new, disease-resistant hybrid will ever have to be replanted or created from the wide variety of genetic material kept there, this will be possible. It's a kind of Noah's Ark for plants in case of disaster.

In Britain, hazelnuts are grown extensively in Kent, including a special type called cobnuts. These are eaten green and immature, when the shell is still soft enough to remove easily with your teeth. They're actually very different in taste from the hard, mature nut – sort of starchy and vegetal, rather than oily and nutty.

Hazelnuts were eaten not only in Saxon times, but pre-historically throughout northern Europe, and archaeological sites always turn up hazelnut remains. So too did work on Britain's original Globe Theatre of Shakespearean fame. Early seventeenth-century theatre-goers were apparently sold hazelnuts to chomp on while they watched plays, and they tossed the shells on the floor. Remember Queen Mab's chariot in *Romeo and Juliet*, fashioned from a hazelnut shell? The audience must have understood that reference immediately just by looking down. So too would it have understood the passage in *The Taming of the Shrew*, when Petruchio claims sarcastically that everyone has been lying about Kate. She doesn't limp, and in fact: 'Kate like the hazel-twig / Is straight and slender and as brown in hue / As hazel nuts, and sweeter than the kernels.'

As for hazel twigs, they have magical properties. Mercury carries one replete with wings and twined with serpents. This is

Botanical print
of a twig from
the hazelnut tree.

the Caduceus – not to be confused with the staff of Asclepius, the symbol of medicine, which only has one serpent and no wings. People have historically confused them anyway, going back to the Middle Ages, probably because Hermes (alias Mercury) was also associated with Hermetic arts like alchemy and the occult – the investigation of unseen things. These arts included healing, hence the use of the symbol for medicine down to this day. Hazel rods, forked ones in particular, are also used in dowsing, or finding subterranean water and precious metals. The 'Y'-shaped divining rod magically points to whatever you are looking for, including buried treasure.

Of course, hazelnuts are also a wonderful cooking ingredient. They appear in biscuits and chocolates, basically just as they are. However, when they are pounded something strange and miraculous happens. A buttery paste is formed that has the same melting point as the temperature of the human mouth, a property shared with few other ingredients, chocolate among them. A mixture of hazelnut paste and chocolate is, in fact, combined to make *gianduja*, originating in Piemonte, Italy. It is named after a commedia dell'arte character, *Gian d'la duja*, or John of the Pots – a merry fellow in a tricorn hat who likes drinking, eating and beautiful women. It is most easily found under the brand name Nutella, and goes well with anything.

Gianduja is used in cakes, and it is a flavouring in gelato in Italy; there are even liqueurs that capture its essence. Yet one could easily argue that sublimated hazelnuts take the form of the liqueur Frangelico, also from Piedmont and reputed to have been invented by monks, hence the name Fra Angelico, though not, they claim, the same monk as the Renaissance painter. It is sweet and tastes intensely of hazelnuts, but also has hints of chocolate and vanilla. There are similar French liqueurs, usually called *noisette*, which is just the word for hazelnut.

The Medieval Almond

The real heyday of nut cookery occurred during the Middle Ages up to the Renaissance. No nut was more beloved than the almond, which featured in a remarkable array of recipes. Almond milk was a substitute for real dairy milk and related products during Lent and other fast days. For much of northern Europe it was an exotic and expensive import worthy of royal tables and very clearly a mark of status, much like imported spices. Serving a dish laden with almonds or laced with almond milk was de rigeur for the fashionable medieval household.

To give an indication of how important almonds were to medieval diners, consider that in 1372, upon the death of Jeanne d'Evreux, the third wife of King Charles iv of France, an inventory was made of her possessions. It is one of the most detailed lists of household goods from that period and includes remarkable luxury items like Chinese porcelain and illustrated prayer books, as well as kitchen equipment and spices. Modern historians cite this inventory to show how highly spices were esteemed, and indeed it includes 6 lb of pepper, 23½ lb of ginger and 13½ lb of cinnamon, as well as more obscure spices that have since disappeared from European cuisine. It also mentions three 'bales' of almonds, which by some estimates weighed the equivalent of 500 pounds. Admittedly, a royal household fed many retainers and servants, but the scale of its provision of almonds, and their inclusion among spices, clearly suggest that they were highly prized.[7]

There survives an almost exactly contemporaneous cookbook from this very court, written by a chef named Guillaume Tirel, better known as Taillevent. His nickname means 'wind-slicer', and was perhaps given to him because of how he brandished his kitchen knives. In any case, from this cookbook we get an excellent idea of how almonds were used. They were cooked with chicken and cumin, and made into almond-milk soups, free-standing, multicoloured almond moulds and the universally popular blancmange – a smooth, white concoction of almond milk, chicken, sugar and rosewater. In other words, almonds were a major ingredient in general use in all types of recipe, not merely in desserts and snacks, or as an incidental garnish. They are found everywhere, and took centre stage in dishes for fast days, when dairy products were forbidden.

Physicians and clergymen also offered ebullient praise for almonds. St Anthony of Padua, when writing about holy epiphanies, described tears of contrition and stated that 'this fluid is the refection for sins, just as almond milk is the diet for the infirmed'. It was so universally understood in the thirteenth century that almond milk nourished invalids, that it served as a metaphor for spiritual nourishment and recovery.

Cooking is really where the almond takes centre stage, and the use of almonds in savoury dishes, as well as in many sweets like marzipan, was heavily influenced by Muslim civilization, just as was the use of spices, sugar, rosewater and citrus fruits. Almond milk, on the other hand, might be a European invention, and of course the religious motivation for its use would be absent among Muslims.

Precise identification of ingredients in old recipes often depends on their translation. The following text gives almond milk as the nut ingredient, but it might just be ground almonds. The recipe is for *sitt al-nawba* from the *Kanz al-Fawa'id fi tanwi al-mawaid* (The Treasure of Useful Advice for the Composition of the Varied Table), compiled in Syria in the thirteenth century. It is for a dish made with a parboiled chicken, fried in sesame oil, to which is added almond milk, made from ground, soaked and strained blanched almonds. The almond milk is cooked down with sugar, and the chicken is served on top of the sauce, garnished with jujubes and raisins soaked in rosewater and musk. Whether the technique was borrowed by Europeans from Baghdad cookbooks is impossible to say, but there are definite lines of affinity between the two cuisines.

Almond products as a substitute for dairy ones are the first to appear in European cookbooks. In fact they appear in the very earliest surviving medieval European cookbook, known as the *Libellus de Arte Coquinaria* (Little Book of Cookery). The original manuscript, which was probably in Latin or French, has been lost. Surprisingly, the cookbook survives in four versions, one in Low German, two in Danish and one in Icelandic. Whoever translated these almost certainly intended the recipes

A decorative wooden nutcracker from the former Yugoslavia.

to be used, even if only by the wealthy, which is at least indirect evidence that almonds had reached the far corners of Western Europe and beyond by the twelfth or thirteenth century. Among the first recipes is one for almond oil. The word 'meat' in the recipe below in Danish, as in medieval English, merely means all foods rather than flesh. Almond oil was thus considered a condiment, appropriate for Lent.

One shall take almond kernels and let them in hot water until the scales [peel] from them come, and cloth [dry] and stamp them in a mortar; and wring them through the cloth. This oil is good for all meats.[8]

The book also contains recipes for almond milk and butter. Almond milk is made by pounding almonds, soaking them in hot water, then straining them. It tastes remarkably like cow's milk, without the toasty almond flavouring one finds in commercial almond milk; the flavouring is extracted from bitter almonds. Almond milk is extraordinarily versatile in the kitchen. Almond butter is made from almond milk in exactly the same way that cheese is made from milk, or tofu from soy, by heating it, then hanging it in a cloth bag to drain. Even an imitation thick sour milk, or curd, is made by combining almond milk with vinegar and cooking this.

For the full efflorescence of almond cookery, we must move to the latter fourteenth and fifteenth centuries, precisely in the time of a demographic slump following the bubonic

Chopping nuts by hand gives them a coarse, uneven texture ideal for cooking.

plague, when almonds, spices and exotic luxuries began to come into more widespread use among the general populace. This was because there were fewer people, and there was more expendable income among those aspiring to eat like their social superiors. It may also account for the proliferation of cookbooks, copies of which circulated among the slightly less affluent than royalty and nobility, who wished to entertain in grand style.

A good illustration of this comes in the form of an English cookbook that survives in some 40 different manuscript versions, best known as *The Forme of Cury*, dating from the late fourteenth century. Cury in this period means cookery, not to be confused with the Indian curry dish.

The original recipe collection was associated with the court of King Richard II, who – while not being remembered for his talent as a ruler – was definitely known for the grandeur of his court and kitchens. The book contains literally dozens of recipes that include almonds. There is a Creme of Almaundes curdled with vinegar, sweetened with sugar and drained until thick. This is then cooled and sliced before service. There is also a fascinating Sawse Sarzyne (Saracen sauce), which at least claims Arab origins. It is made with rosehips, and blanched and fried almonds pounded in a mortar, moistened with wine, sweetened with sugar and spiced, then thickened with rice starch and coloured with alkanet – a red powdered dye made from the roots of *Alkanna tinctoria*. It is suggested that it be served with shredded capon garnished with pomegranate seeds. This is a typically medieval dish in combining sweet, spicy and savoury flavours as well as being coloured. Almonds are used in gruel, with ground herbs, in a dish called Iowtes or Jutes, in saffron-laden soups, with kid in a stew, with salmon in an almond sauce called Vyaunde Cypre, and with oysters. There is literally no culinary context in which almonds do not figure, but they appear especially in Lenten dishes. Here is a recipe for a kind of pie, 'Leche frys in lentoun' – 'leche' merely means to slice. Here the 'coffin' means a pie crust; it was used as a container, but not eaten, and contained no butter as this was a dish for Lent. The þ symbol is a thorn, which simply denotes *th*. 'Canel' means canella, a kind of cinnamon, and 'gode powdours' is a spice mix. 'Saundres' is powdered sandalwood, which was used as a red dye. To farce means to stuff.

> Leche frys in lentoun. Drawe a thik almaunde mylke wiþ water. Take dates and pyke hem clene with apples and peeres, & mynce hem with prunes damysyns; take out þe stones out of þe prunes, & kerve the prunes a two. Do þereto raisouns coraunce, sugur, flour of canel, hoole macys and clowes, gode powdours & salt; color hem up with saundres. Meng þise with oile. Make a coffyn as thou didest bifore & do þis fars therin, & bake it wel, and serve it forth.[9]

In the *Diversa Cibaria*, a related English manuscript of the same type, sixteen of the first 23 recipes include almond milk. They are contained in dishes with such diverse ingredients as capon, strawberries, eggs with ginger, and even turbot or eels. Again, the principal use of almonds is in savoury dishes, though there is no real distinction between main courses and sweet desserts, as many of these recipes also contain sugar.

The French were equally enthusiastic about almond milk, and once again Taillevent is the best source for recipes. His *Viandier* includes a number of internationally known recipes, including a *comminee d'amandes*, or cumin-flavoured dish. This is basically a chicken cooked in water, quartered and fried in lard. To this are added ground almonds, broth for moistening and the cooked meat. The flavouring comes from ginger

Limbourg Brothers, 'November', from *Très Riches Heures du Duc de Berry*, 1412–16. This illumination shows the month when pigs are let run wild in the forest to feed on mast.

and cumin infused in wine and verjus. Taillevent also has a dish called 'garlins', or in some manuscripts 'taillis' (meaning sliced), which is figs and raisins with almond milk, boiled together, into which go cracknels (wafers), galettes (crêpes) and bread crusts cut small, with saffron and sugar. The ingredients are cooked together until thick, then the garlins is sliced and put into bowls.

Taillevent additionally has a recipe for a multicoloured blancmange in which ground almonds are boiled and thickened with beaten rice or starch. The mixture is split into several parts, and each part is separately coloured with alkanet, tournesoc (orchil lichen), azure and parsley. The colours are saturated into lard with salt and sugar.

The standard blancmange was specifically intended for invalids. It was among the most popular of all medieval recipes, and though it varied from cookbook to cookbook, it was usually made up of a combination of parboiled capon or chicken shredded and pounded smooth, and almond milk, rice flour, rosewater and sugar, which was cooked until thick. In the end it resembled a thick chicken pudding, perhaps strange to our sensibilities, admittedly, though adored by medieval diners. The name means 'white food', and the ingredients were thought to be both highly nutritious and easy to digest, hence the association with delicate constitutions. The dish, strangely enough, survives today as blancmange, a sweet almond confection without the capon.

Not surprisingly, almonds also figure widely in regions where they are grown, though perhaps without as much social clout. The anonymous Catalan *Llibre de sent soví*, also of the late fourteenth or early fifteenth century, contains a number of arresting and innovative recipes. The following recipe is remarkable for the technique, and it should be noted that the bain-marie first became popular in writings by medieval alchemists such as Raymond Llul, from this very region. Here it is used to gently cook beans without letting them burn. The recipe is for tender fava beans in almond milk.

> If you want to make tender favas in almond milk, you do it thus: Take the favas, and boil them well in hot water, until they are cooked. Then get almond milk, and put them covered in the milk with oil and salt, and place this in a hot bain-marie of boiling water. And when they are cooked add parsley, basil and marjoram and other good spices, and a bit of ginger, and some vinegar.[10]

Another Catalan cookbook was written sometime in the early fifteenth century at the Aragonese court in Naples by one Rupert of Nola. It was printed in 1520, and subsequently in Castilian translation in 1525. Almonds are used in it no less than they were in earlier medieval texts. The recipe section contains Rupert's version of the blancmange recipe mentioned above. In many respects the detailed instructions and measurements suggest that the text is not written for a professional chef, but for someone unfamiliar with basic techniques, perhaps a home cook. Revealingly, this recipe appears to have been adapted by Martino of Como (see below), who streamlined and clarified the instructions, and removed all the details in procedure such as butchering and being careful not to let the pot burn, suggesting that his text was indeed written for professionals.

The Italians were equally heavy handed with almonds in their cookery. This recipe comes from Venice and probably dates to the early fifteenth century. It is for a sweet-and-sour sauce typical of the region, and its title is still sometimes used in Venetian dialect today. The cookbook is merely known as *Anonimo Veneziano* (Anonymous Venetian).

A Cesame of whatever fish you want

Take the fish and fry it, take onions and boil them a little
and chop them finely, then fry well. Then take vinegar and
water and whole cleaned almonds, and raisins, strong
spices, and a little honey, and let everything boil together
and put it over the fish.[11]

Cookbooks of the latter part of the fifteenth century are
no less enthusiastic about almonds than earlier ones, but the
significant difference between cookbooks of the two periods
was that in the later period they were printed and often translated or written in the vernacular. Recipes thus reached a
much wider audience. The first printed cookbook, *De honesta
voluptate* (On Honest Pleasure), printed in Rome in about
1470, is actually a hybrid, a combination of a mid-fifteenth-
century cookbook written by Martino of Como that survives
in several manuscript versions, stuffed into a scholarly work
about diet and natural history by Bartolomeo Sacchi, better
known as Platina, the first librarian of the Vatican Library.
Within the next century, Platina's text was translated into Italian,
French, German and Dutch, and partially into English.

The text contains not only a general discussion about
almonds, but 57 almond recipes. The general trend was to move
away from almond milk as the prime ingredient, and to incorporate almonds themselves into more dishes and confections.
For example, Platina notes that almonds are commonly candied
in melted sugar, and served as a comfit at the end of a meal.
Comfits, interestingly, were eaten for both pleasure and health;
sugar was considered one of the best of foods, and it figures
largely in most recipes, even savoury ones. Platina's main entry
for almonds also reveals the broadening use of almonds. He explains that people eat them 'too greedily', green and immature,

H. Lalo's *Amandines de Provence Biscuits*, poster, early 1900s.

and this can cause headaches, but that bitter ones have many medicinal uses. Peeled almonds and sugar with butter in prepared dishes are good for counteracting phlegm, and relieve a cold and dry cough. As food, sweet almonds were eaten both by themselves and mixed into dishes in the second and third courses. That is, they were served both along with main courses and in the final course with fruits, but not (revealingly) at the start of a meal, and presumably this recommendation has a medicinal logic: the astringency of almonds being better to close the mouth of the stomach toward the end of the meal to facilitate digestion.

The recipes, taken from Martino's cookbook, are filled with almonds and almond products, and this may very well be the most amygdalophilic cookbook ever written. Many of the almond recipes have earlier antecedents, including the blancmange mentioned above, and a few seem to be direct adaptations of Catalan recipes in Rupert's cookbook. For example, a Catalan Mirause (meaning half-roast) includes a semi-roasted capon or chicken, cut up and put into a pot. Next are added grated almonds that have been toasted under warm ashes and cleaned with a linen cloth. Toasted bread is added as a thickener, with vinegar and broth, and this is strained, then cinnamon, ginger and a good deal of sugar are added and the mixture is cooked long on a slow fire, while stirring with a spoon. Platina adds that he has never eaten anything more pleasant, and provides medical advice to the effect that it is very nourishing, slowly digested, heats the liver and kidneys, makes body fat and 'incites venus' – that is, serves as an aphrodisiac.

Martino has a number of intriguing new recipes as well. His white broth consists of a pound of almonds peeled and pounded, then sprinkled with water so that the oil remains in suspension. Twenty egg whites are added, as well as softened breadcrumbs, verjuice, white ginger and broth. This mixture is then strained into a pot and cooked further. There is also rice cooked with almonds and sugar, and as a porridge. There is, however, nothing more inventive than the shells of fava beans stuffed with a paste of ground almonds, rosewater and sugar, roasted in a pan, then covered with broth and served

A fresh pesto made with basil, garlic, pine nuts and oil. In the Middle Ages it was made with a wide variety of herbs and nuts.

with a flourish of parsley and spices. This is the epitome of late-medieval cuisine, a 'subtlety', as it would have been called in English, designed to titillate and surprise diners. What they see is a lowly peasant fava dish, but it turns out to be almonds in disguise.

Martino's almond fritters sound delicious – they include ground almonds, rosewater, boiled chicken breast pounded separately, flour, egg whites and sugar, fried in lard or oil. There are many other fritters containing almonds, employing rice, figs and almonds, that are made into the shapes of fish. The variety and novelty of these recipes shows a cook willing to experiment with an ingredient in ways that compare favourably with anything being done by modern chefs. Almonds are combined with prunes in a sauce called *tuccetum*, with pomegranates and dates in a Persian *moretum*, akin to a pesto, and there is something that comes very close to a modern pesto, made with garlic and almonds. One can even imagine the modern romesco sauce to be a descendant of these sauces once chilli peppers and tomatoes are added.

Martino also highlights many dishes with almonds as the main ingredient. There is a *mandorlata*, or as Platina latinizes it, *amygdalinum*, a kind of white gazpacho. In another similar dish for Lent, orange juice and saffron are used rather than broth. There is a Lenten blancmange based on fish and pea broth, which bears mentioning if only for the proportions, including a pound and a half of almonds. Almonds figure in sweets such as a marzipan tart, almond jellies, an artifical almond ricotta and almond custard pies. Clearly it is interest in almonds themselves that inspired these remarkable recipes.

Almonds were not only beloved of southern Europeans. The *Keukenboek*, published in Ghent in modern-day Belgium, offers many almond recipes, including an almond pudding and almond milk sweetened with sugar. Almonds still supplied the principal substitute for dairy products on Catholic fast days, which must have been difficult in a region heavily committed to cattle rearing. The following imitation cheese shows how almonds could be used even in a fairly modest household.

> Butter and Cheese from almonds – You make good almond milk, then boil that in a pan with good wine vinegar in a ladle, just a little all together, and once the milk begins to curdle, then draw the curds back and take a little straw basket lined with a cloth, there let the curds cool, and have a clean cheese mold and mix in there sugar with the curds, make cheese in the cheese mold and butter on a plate.[12]

Sixteenth-century authors also used almonds extensively, but it seems as though recipes in which they were used steadily declined after the Middle Ages. It might be simply that during the Reformation Lenten rules were gradually abandoned so that regular milk could be used whenever one liked in northern Europe. Even in southern Europe, the restrictions seem to have loosened so that butter, milk and cream were used more often, rather than almond milk. Still, nuts have their place in modern cookery, too, more often as a health food than one utilized during fasting and penitence.

Modern 'Raw Food'

It is of course ironic that products like almond milk have once again popped up on supermarket shelves, with explicit health claims and specifically for people who want to avoid animal products, though admittedly for very different reasons than in the past. I think raw-food advocates are probably the greatest promoters of nut cookery today.

By pure coincidence, while I was writing this book my wife was drawn very much into the raw-food movement. Being addicted to cooking with heat I was at first sceptical, though in my view some foods are indeed better raw and unprocessed, like salad vegetables when fresh and crunchy, fish always, meat often. Sure, some foods are simply better unprocessed. All things are good when they leave the hands of the creator, but degenerate in the hands of man, to paraphrase Rousseau. So maybe not cooking food would be an interesting gastronomic exercise.

But raw does not mean unprocessed. Nor does it include raw meat. It should more properly be called the 'vegan, grain- and gluten-free and even soy-free, raw diet, which requires a lot of big noisy machines to make'. Think of juice blends made from kale, apples and turnips. For these, you need a heavy-duty juice machine to shred and spin or squeeze the juice out of the vegetables and fruits, leaving behind pulp and fibre, which I thought was good for you. Anyway, nuts are absolutely central to this diet, or let us call it a cuisine. There are not only

A curious nut cracker in the form of an animal head, Italian, late 17th century, steel and brass.

restaurants that serve raw food, but also many cookbooks with recipes for raw hamburgers (again no meat), chilli and chips, and bread and pizza. I'm not sure why they replicate this kind of food instead of creating entirely new raw dishes, but some of this stuff tastes quite good, and it definitely takes a lot of imagination to create it.

Apart from juicers, food processors are useful, as are dehydrators. Drying foods is OK – just not cooking them. I'm anticipating that molecular gastronomy equipment and its tricks will soon migrate into the raw field, too, since these are the two most technologically plugged-in cuisines of today. Imagine pomegranate and spinach alginate beads, or centrifuged flax foam.

As far as raw-food cuisine is concerned, nuts as used in it take on whole new forms, and even take centre stage in a way they never would in trendy molecular restaurants, or in any other cuisine for that matter. First of all, they pretty much hold everything together, ground up, soaked or mixed into other foods for texture. The milk, not just of almonds, but of absolutely any other nut, is made into sauces that are really delectable. For examples, see the instructions for Sundried Tomato Quick Cashew Cheese and Spinach Cracker Bread in the recipe section.

4
Nuts Familiar and Exotic

Hickory and Pecan

People who live in eastern North America may have seen hickory nuts on the ground, but not many have eaten them. They are in the genus *Carya*, and are classified as a drupe because they grow in a thick outer husk that starts out green, then turns brown and splits open when mature. Otherwise they are perfectly nut-like inside. Hickory nuts and walnuts are called *tryma*, which means a hole, and derives from the Greek words for 'to wear away', which is sort of what the husk does when it is ready to eat. Few people do eat them nowadays and there is no commercial production, with the exception of one species, *C. illinoinensis*, alias the pecan (see below).

There are many distinct species of hickory nut, most of which are native to the U.S. There is the pignut (which tastes awful), shagbark, mockernut and nutmeg hickory. When Americans hear the word hickory, apart from visualizing smoked hams, they might think of Old Hickory himself. This was President Andrew Jackson, who got the nickname from the wood, not the nut. The wood is just about as hard and tough as wood gets, so much so that it makes great baseball bats and golf-club shafts. Actually the nickname is strangely ironic, because the Creek Indians, whom Jackson pretty much

A pecan seller in rural Georgia, early 20th century.

destroyed, lived on hickory nuts. John Bartram, writing in 1792, said that the Creeks pounded up the nuts, then boiled them and finally strained off the milk, which is as sweet and rich as fresh cream. The milk was called *powcohicoria* in the Algonkian language, and this is where the word hickory comes from. The Creeks used the milk in dishes with corn and hominy – that is until Jackson defeated them and pushed the survivors to the west, along with most other tribes in the south. Consider for a moment the rare coincidence of similarity between this sweet, nutty corn mixture and the medieval-era Lenten puddings made with almond milk and rice. They actually coexisted on either side of the Atlantic.

The pecan is another native American nut. Pecans are the most familiar nuts in the *Carya* genus, and they are just about as good as a nut can get. We get the word directly from Native American languages: *paccan* in Algonkian, for example, meaning a nut that needs to be cracked with a stone. They are native to a long swathe of land extending from Illinois down through Missouri, Arkansas, Louisiana, Oklahoma and Texas, straight down into Mexico. The roots of the pecan industry are said to originate in the experiments of an African slave in Vachery, Louisiana, on the Oak Alley plantation. There one Antoine, in 1847, succeeded in grafting pecans, which normally would not come true to seed if the nuts were planted. Only in the later nineteenth century were they grown commercially, and most are grown today in Georgia, though they were introduced there.

A wide disparity separates the pronunciation of the word pecan as well. Southerners, who include people in southern New Jersey, might pronounce it pe-KAHN, but a few miles to the north it is PEE-can, which of course sounds ridiculous to a Southerner. Yet I have heard people like the Southern food TV star Paula Deen call it a PEE-can. Pecan pie is quite simply the best pie on Earth, provided it's not too sweet. The old recipe for it is not actually very old, with some claiming that it dates

Whole pecans in the shell only became a cultivated crop relatively recently.

A traditional American pecan pie is a standard for Thanksgiving and other holidays.

back to 1925, when corn syrup manufacturers introduced it. Earlier recipes were quite different, usually just involving pecans boiled in milk, added to custard and topped with meringue.[1] The real thing must be dense and laden with dark Blue Label Karo corn syrup. It is basically composed of just 2 eggs, 1 cup (240 ml) syrup, 1 cup (200 g) sugar, 1 cup (115 g) crushed pecans, and 2 tablespoons melted butter, with some vanilla, mixed and baked in a pie shell. The top should be laden with whole nuts, too. With these basic ingredients, you can also experiment – decrease the level of sugar, or substitute it with maple syrup, and add more butter and maybe a little cinnamon. They may call you a heretic, but it's worth taking that chance.

Pine Nuts

Pine nuts are not exclusively American. Asia has its own species that flourish in Korea, China and Siberia. The Mediterranean

A pine cone, originally called a pine 'apple', with its nuts.

has the stone pine (*Pinus pinea*), yielding pignoli. But the most interesting pine-nut story comes from the American southwest. For millennia, pine trees provided food for Native American peoples – especially the pinyon or piñon pine (*P. edulis*), from which are harvested what were simply called Indian nuts when I was young. They were small, beige, hard shelled and always sold in the shell. You could spend many hours just cracking them one by one with your teeth. You don't see them around much anymore, and for very good reason. The land on which they grow, only in the wild, which is mostly federal or state forests, has since the 1960s been increasingly devoted to cattle rearing. The pine trees have been cut down to grow pasture for the cattle. These new grasslands are much more susceptible to wildfires than the trees were, and also don't hold water as well. What once worked very well ecologically to feed the birds, squirrels and people, is now devoted mostly to growing beef.

In places such as Santa Fe, New Mexico, there are people selling pine nuts on the street, though they are outrageously expensive, especially in years when the crops are small. They are well worth it, make no mistake. The cost comes from the difficulty involved in harvesting them. Firstly, the trees only bear good crops every five years. Secondly, Native Americans have the rights to harvest them, but others must bid to do so in a kind of lottery. If they win, they have to take their long poles fitted with hooks or claws, knock off the pine cones, sack them up, wait until they open, then separate the nuts from the cones. The whole process is simply not well suited to becoming a large-scale business, which is why American pine nuts are becoming increasingly hard to find.

There are also trees in the Sierras, bearing darker and longer shelled nuts. You get sticky sap all over yourself if you even touch them, but it's still worth it. On the Nevada side you will even find the Pine Nut Mountains, though most of the trees on them were cleared in the nineteenth century and turned into charcoal, used in the smelting of silver ore. So all that ephemeral wealth that came out of the Comstock

Cold pine-nut soup is made by simply pounding the nuts and adding water and seasoning. See recipe, p. 106.

A variety of nuts for sale in a market in Dunhuang, Gansu province, China.

Lode was at the cost of a renewable natural resource – and a delicious one to boot.

All this explains why most pine nuts imported into the u.s. now come from China. They are also shelled, simply to reduce shipping costs, and are consequently often rancid. You can find Italian pine nuts, sometimes sold in tiny jars along with spices, for upwards of $10; these have probably been on the shelf for years. You might be able to make a dozen biscuits with a little jar like this. If you are very lucky you may be able to find the large green pine cones (the original pine apples, by the way) that are sometimes imported from Italy. You bake them to release the nuts – and these are without doubt the tastiest that can be found.

Chinese pine nuts are not necessarily bad, though a few years ago many people, including myself, experienced what is now known as pine mouth. I was in Boston teaching a food-history class that included cooking and tasting pine nuts, and everything tasted bitter and metallic. It was a nightmare and lasted for about two weeks. No one knows for sure what caused this, but the pine nuts were probably from a different species of pine to standard pine nuts, imported when there were low supplies from the regular sources. There are no laws that require importers to denote which species of pine they are importing, though I suspect after a lot of bad publicity importers are now being more careful.

Whatever type you use, pine nuts lend themselves to cooking extraordinarily well. Pesto is the most famous recipe in which pine nuts are used, and in my view should never be made in a blender or food processor, but rather as it has been since antiquity, in a mortar with a pestle (hence the name pesto). If you are lucky enough to eat pesto in Genoa, Italy, where they use a tiny-leaved basil, a good handful of pine nuts, a little garlic, sweet olive oil, Parmigiano cheese and nothing else, you will notice that a ladleful of hot water from the pasta serves to make a smooth emulsion of the sauce, so that it is not completely raw.

The pine-nut pesto is not the only pesto, classic or otherwise. Hundreds of years ago there was a whole tribe of pounded sauces like this, made with parsley or other herbs, walnuts and basically whatever struck the fancy. Take, for example, Bartolomeo Stefani's recipe from 1662, which would today be decried as heresy.

Sapore d'erbe odorifere (Sauce of aromatic herbs)

Take marjoram, basil, parsley for each serving, one ounce of anise, two ounces of cleaned pistachios, four slices of bread soaked in rose vinegar, and sprinkle with vinegar, pound all the aforesaid in a mortar, with two ounces of fine sugar, temper with a little vinegar and the juice of two lemons, and it makes a very pleasing and tasty little sauce.[2]

A cup of freshly shelled pine nuts, wonderful toasted and added to salads.

Pine nuts are often paired with raisins – and not only in sweets. In fact, pine nuts with capers, anchovies, a pinch of cinnamon and a touch of vinegar combine in a magnificent way, creating not a harmony of flavours, but a complex counterpoint of savoury, sweet, bitter, sour, salty and aromatic sensations. The combination makes one think of Sicily, but the origin of this flavour combination is in the Arab world, which ruled over Sicily from the mid-tenth to the mid-eleventh century.

Among the stranger opinions one will find among authorities of the past is that pine nuts, in the words of the physician Antonius Gazius of Padua, Italy, writing in 1491, 'augment coitus', especially when eaten with the whitest kind of sugar, called *tabarzet*.[3] That is they are not exactly an aphrodisiac, but they aid in conception. Normally anything nourishing and easy to digest would fall into this category among early modern physicians, and pine nuts were considered hot and dry and quite nourishing. Modern commentators usually mention zinc, which is necessary for manufacturing testosterone, but clearly there must have been some other logic informing earlier opinion. I suspect it was the doctrine of signatures, whereby the shape, colour or other attribute reveals a plant's medicinal virtues. The colour of pine nuts, and above all their aroma, are distinctly reminiscent of human seed. In the same way that wine is good for generating blood, and meat for building flesh, pine nuts might be just the thing for reproduction.

Exotic Nuts of Hunters and Gatherers

Perhaps it should come as no surprise that the few people left in the world who are still hunters and gatherers make greater use of nuts as a central part of their diet than any other societies. Examples of such nuts – both familiar and less so – are described here.

Macadamias

The macadamia nut comes from two trees in the genus *Macadamia*. (The nuts of most *Macadamia* species are in fact not edible and contain cyanogenic glycosides, which turn to cyanide in the body if ingested.) The macadamia nut is not only truly exotic, but indeed the hardest nut to crack. That is, not only is its shell almost completely impenetrable, even resisting a good swing with a sledge hammer, but its fascinating origin makes it one of the best articles of food-history trivia. My students always initially think that it originates from Hawaii, where it is widely grown today. Then someone suggests South

America, India or Africa. 'Think of the name', I say. 'MacAdam. Scotland?' They are actually named after Dr John Macadam, a Scottish chemist and physician transplanted to Australia. The botanist Ferdinand von Mueller named the genus after his friend Macadam, 'the talented and deserving secretary of our institute' (the Philosophic Institute of Victoria, later called the Royal Society). The discoverer of the macadamia nut in 1828, however, was botanist-explorer Allan Cunningham, though the first specimen appears to have been collected by Ludwig Leichart in 1843. Aboriginal Australians had, of course, been eating macadamia nuts for some time – 40,000 years or thereabout, since they first arrived in Australia. Of all the many plants they consumed, no other has become a domesticated commercial crop, the charming wattleseeds of Australian acacias notwithstanding.

Cultivation of macadamia nuts began when one Walter Hill planted macadamia trees in 1858 in the Botanic Gardens

Macadamia nuts are among the hardest on earth, resisting even the blow of a hammer.

in Brisbane. The story goes that at first he thought the nuts were poisonous, until he found an assistant munching away on them with no ill effect. After a few days without the boy dropping dead, he was convinced that they could be used for food; he tasted them and proclaimed them to be excellent, and eventually orchards were planted in New South Wales.

The American botanist Luther Burbank regarded the macadamia as the world's best eating nut, and by the 1870s the nuts were grown experimentally at Berkeley at the College of Agriculture, in the USA. There are a few macadamia-nut growers in California today, mostly in San Diego and Santa Barbara, where there are never frosts, and there are even some in places like Florida, Kenya and Guatemala. Hawaii has of course become this nut's second home. William H. Purvis, a sugar-plantation manager, brought seeds to Hawaii in the 1880s, but it was not until the early nineteenth century that the agricultural experiment station began tests to establish an industry. They figured out how to graft the trees and acre upon acre was planted. So readily is Hawaii identified with the nut today that Honolulu Airport is stacked with jars of salted Mauna Loa nuts and boxes of chocolate-covered macadamias for tourists to take home.

Many other Australian nuts are considered to be good 'bush tucker', like the Johnstone River almond (*Elaeocarpus bancroftii*), kurrajong (*Brachychiton populneus*), red bopple (*Hicksbeachia pinnatifolia*), yellow walnut (*Beilschmiedia bancroftii*), burrawang (*Macrozamia communis*) and bunya (*Araucaria bidwillii*). For the most part it is Aboriginal peoples who make use of these, which perhaps supports the idea that the less tainted people are by civilization, the greater is their dependence on wild nuts. Examples from hunters and gatherers around the world seem to bear out this idea.

Mongongo

The Mongongo tree (*Schinziophyton rautanenii*), sometimes called the manketti, grows in the Kalahari Desert in Namibia and Botswana, and has been a favoured food of San bushmen for at least the past seven millennia. It constitutes a third of their caloric intake, and must be regarded as the staple of their diet. In fact, when asked why they remain hunters and gatherers instead of becoming farmers, their stock reply is, 'When there are so many mongongo nuts in the world, why would anyone plant crops?' The fruits of this tree are collected, the outer husk is removed and the sweet flesh is eaten dried or boiled into a kind of porridge. Inside are the hard nuts, which can be roasted in a pile of hot sand, cracked open and eaten. The most remarkable thing about these nuts is the method of gathering. They can be collected from the ground, but are also gathered from piles of elephant dung since the nut passes through the animal whole. The nuts contain a great deal of oil, which is featured in New Age skin-care products.

Cashews

The cashew comes from a tree (*Anacardium occidentale*) that grows widely in tropical climates. It might not seem very exotic, but stop to consider that it comes from equatorial Brazil and is shaped like no other nut, and that its fruit is completely unknown outside the regions in which it grows. This is the upside-down, heart-shaped, reddish or yellow cashew 'apple' that is made into jam or juice, or even fermented into alcohol. The plant gets its genus name, *Anacardium*, from the fruit, which translates as 'upside-down heart', which it indeed

Cashew nut factory, Nitte, India.

resembles. The nut sticks out beneath the fruit like a sore thumb, something like a cedilla (ç). There's a story told in Sri Lanka that after God had created the Earth, the devil felt left out and wanted to make something. He went away and came up with this fruit. God took one look at it and said that the devil had forgotten to include the seed. Well, the devil said, I'll just stick it on the outside here, hence the absurd position. Actually the fruit is a swollen stem; the nut is the true fruit, the shell of which is a powerful skin irritant, being related to poison ivy. Even smelling the smoke from roasting the shells can cause burning sensations.

The name 'cashew' comes from the Tupi language – *acajú*. The Portuguese who encountered it in the sixteenth century immediately brought it to their colonies around the world: to Mozambique, to Goa and southeast India, and to Malacca on the Malay peninsula; the Spanish brought it to the Philippines.

Today Nigeria, Vietnam and India produce most of the world's cashews. It's a pity that most people in the West only encounter cashews in salted nut mixes. Ground cashews make a marvellous thickener for curries. They can also be soaked and strained to make milk and a kind of cheese. Cashew butter is becoming increasingly common on food-shop shelves, though it is very easy to make at home simply by pounding or processing the nuts into a spreadable paste with a little salt and oil.

Paradise Nut

There are some nuts that are so exotic that few people have ever seen them except where they grow. One can only wonder about the flavour of the paradise nut (*Lecythis zabucajo*), which grows in Guiana and Venezuela. The nut grows in a big, hard, acorn-shaped capsule with a detachable lid, similar to a Brazil nut, in which it is neatly arranged and attached to a white aril. Paradise nuts are also called monkey pots, and it's easy to imagine a little furry simian gingerly picking out the nuts.

Yeheb

Another oddity is the yeheb (or ye'eb, or yicib, *Cordeauxia edulis*) found in Somalia, which grows on an evergreen shrub in the dry near-desert. It's quite rare nowadays and endangered, because camels and goats like to eat the plants in the dry season (they are said to give their flesh an incomparable flavour). Interestingly, the leaves yield a deep-red dye and harvesting them leaves you red-handed. Cattle that graze on the plants also end up with skeletons that are completely red.

Pili nuts.

Karuka

The karuka nut (*Pandanus julianettii*) occurs in the tropical high-lands of Papua New Guinea. It grows in a pointy, finger-length fruit studded in a huge, round cone, which is also eaten. Once removed, the long, hexagonal-shaped nuts are dried and smoked and are a major food source for the local inhabitants. They are said to last for years after smoking.

Pili

Once imported to the U.S. from the Philippines, at a time when it was a colonial possession, the pili nut (*Canarium ovatum*) is no longer available in North America. Imagine that in 1914 the editor of the *Journal of Heredity* could write:

Exotic nuts, hunted and gathered: kukui.

> Following the interest in nuts among consumers . . .
> several new sorts have appeared on the markets of the
> United States, and by their excellence give promise of
> attaining considerable commercial performance. The
> best known of these is probably the pili nut of the Philip-
> pines, which is now commonly sold throughout the
> United States.[4]

Another nut was the paradise nut mentioned above, and yet
another the 'Queensland Nut', now better known as the
macadamia. What happened to the pili nut? It probably failed
in the u.s. due to the difficulty of propagating it and finding a
cultivar that could be grown on a commercial scale.

Pili nuts are still eaten widely in their native habitat, of
course, consumed as a snack and used much like almonds are
used elsewhere. They look something like almonds, but have
pointy ends and extremely hard shells. They are collected and

processed into sweets and ice cream, and crushed for oil; one species of the tree itself yields a gum called *elemi*, which is used to caulk boats. You can find pili nuts for sale online, but once a viable way to plant and process them is developed, it is probable that you will see them alongside every other nut on food-shop shelves once again.

Kukui

The kukui is the official tree of Hawaii, even though it is not indigenous (there are practically no indigenous food plants in Hawaii), but was brought to Hawaii by settlers from Polynesia. The scientific name of the tree is *Aleurites moluccana*, although its likely origin is Malaysia. Remarkably, its nuts contain so much oil that you can stick them on skewers and light them up as candles, hence the name candlenut. Some sources state that kikui are toxic and purgative, and packages in which they are sold do contain stringent warnings. Nonetheless, kikui are commonly roasted and mixed with salt, and perhaps seaweed and chilli, and pounded into a kind of flavouring called *inamona*, which is used on *poke*, the raw-fish dish of Hawaii. In Hawaii, you are likely to find the shells polished and strung on a satin string in the form of a lei, available in just about every gift shop.

5
Nuts in Sweets, Snacks and Junk Food

Pistachios

When I was young I went to summer camp in the Pocono Mountains of Pennsylvania. Among our daily rations we were not furnished with sweets of any kind. There were therefore two options. The first was a 'care package' from home. I only learned years later that this term originally referred to packages of food sent to soldiers abroad, but not usually containing sweets, since chocolate, gum and cigarettes were part of the regular military issue. The other option was Charley's, a gas station maybe half a mile's march from the camp and along a fairly busy highway. We couldn't go on our own, of course, so maybe once a week or two we would trudge single file for our dose of sugary sweets. Charley himself was ancient, had one arm, was as thin as a rail and had a big, broad smile. Watching him bag the sweets and run the cash register with one arm was half the fun. The other half was the decidedly antiquated sweets he carried: Mary Janes – a kind of stale butterscotch taffy – liquorice whips, Good & Plenty, Sugar Daddy, Jujubes, BB Bats – taffy on a stick. Best of them all were the long, slender packets of pistachios dyed red.

Why anyone would dye a perfectly natural food red has always puzzled me. Supposedly this practice was designed to hide imperfections in the cheapest grade of pistachios imported from Iran – then still ruled by the Shah. I think it was simply to amuse children whose fingers and mouths would be stained with a lurid red dye. This was based on coal tar and in 1976, following Soviet tests on laboratory rats, it was declared carcinogenic and removed from the market. Suddenly pistachios and other red-dyed products lost their crimson lustre.

Perhaps not coincidentally, this is exactly when pistachios began to be grown in California and almost exactly when protests against the Shah of Iran escalated and within a few years he was overthrown. As for pistachios, the u.s. industry took off, and suddenly beige shells and greenish-tinged nuts proliferated. The greenish colour is the 'natural' colour of the nuts, though sometimes they are tinged purplish or even red in nature. But green is more typical, so green pistachio ice cream served in Chinese restaurants wasn't so far fetched after all. Even more recently, in 2010, in response to the continuing nuclear programme in Iran, President Barack Obama banned the importation of pistachios into the u.s. The California industry was poised to dominate the market in the usa and there is every indication that it will do so.

Whatever the colour, there is no nut as fun to eat as the pistachio. The nuts beg to be split by the teeth in a way that no other nut can match, and the shells must be spat out with much greater conviction than a wimpy sunflower seed.

Pistachios are an ancient nut, mentioned in the Bible – many translators have rendered the Hebrew word *botnim* (בטנים) as pistachios. In Genesis 43:11, Joseph, now an Egyptian official, gives food to the sons of Jacob who left Canaan during a famine. He secretly slips them some silver, too, but keeps

Simeon as ransom to make sure they are honest men. They are then told to return with their youngest son Benjamin.

Jacob sends his sons back to the Egyptian official with a gift of the best products of the land: balm, honey, gum tragacanth, myrrh, pistachios and almonds. These were all luxury goods, but more importantly, they are exactly what one uses to make sweets. The honey might have been actual bee's honey, but many translate it as a rob, or boiled down grape syrup – what was called *sapa* in ancient Rome. Crush the nuts, add the syrup, thicken the mixture with the gum and perfume it with myrrh, and you have *loukoum*, or what in the West is called Turkish delight. My grandfather (who came from Kastoria in northern Greece) used to buy a big log of it. It was greenish-grey, studded with pistachios and covered in powdered sugar, which went all over the place as you ate it. It usually has a hint of rose, too. It is chewy and sweet and crunchy all at the same time – and nothing like the so-called Turkish delight that comes in brightly coloured squares.

Loukoum or Turkish Delight, a confection studded with pistachios.

There is much disagreement among ancient linguists about a word in Assyrian found in the oldest culinary tablets: *butumtu* or *buttutu*. Some translate it as terebinth – or turpentine tree, which does bear berries; they are very bitter and possibly were intended to be included in one of the recipes. The tree is in the genus *Pistachia*. Others translate the word as pistachio, in which case there is a fabulous recipe from a cuneiform recipe tablet for ground dates perhaps first rolled into a log, then rolled in crushed pistachios. Very similar recipes abound today.

Nuts are incredibly versatile in the kitchen. The most basic way to cook them is to give them a brief toasting to bring out their flavour, just by placing them briefly near a heat source. Putting them on a rock near a fire would be the ideal way to try this gastronomic experiment, but using an iron pan works just as well. Here are just some examples of ways in which walnuts can be used in the kitchen.

Take five raw walnuts. Leave the first raw and taste it: it's fine, but not thrilling. Place the second walnut in a hot pan and toast it for just a minute or so until it is lightly browned. Let it cool and taste it: you will find that it is richer, deeper and denser in flavour than the first walnut. Toast the third walnut and sprinkle it with salt: now some real magic begins to happen. The flavour rounds out and fills your entire mouth. Toast the fourth walnut, sprinkle it with salt and leave it in the pan with a sprinkling of sugar, until the sugar melts, then swirl the pan and nut until the sugary goo sticks to the crevices in the walnut. Remove carefully with a spoon and let cool thoroughly. You have just crossed the threshold into pure deliciousness. Now do the same thing with the fifth walnut, but add cinnamon, chilli pepper or cardamom. Next, substitute pecans. Throw some butter into the mix. You've just invented pralines. Then drizzle or dip these in chocolate. Or

Candied pecans are made by tossing the nuts in melted sugar, spices and salt.

take a whole pound of nuts, coarsely crush them, add butter, sugar and a pinch of salt, put them on a baking sheet, bake until bubbly, then drizzle with chocolate. Let this cool and crack it up before eating it. I dare you to resist eating it all.

Nuts are destined to go into sweets and biscuits – ancient noble confections and modern ones alike – such as marzipan, macaroons, pine-nut-studded biscuits and pecan sandies (a popular American pecan cookie), Mexican wedding cookies, crumbly with crushed walnuts, and perhaps best of all, the chocolate-chip cookie riddled with macadamia nuts. However, no other nut serves as well in cooking as the walnut.

Walnuts

Walnuts are the quintessential nut and they are actually what the word nut refers to etymologically. Say nuts and the walnut comes to mind, perhaps in a Victorian parlour, beside the fire with leather armchairs, a glass of port and a hunk of stilton. Walnuts come from beautiful, tall trees from which the walnuts hang like little green tennis balls, eventually turning dark brown. In Britain they are picked green, traditionally on 15 June – the feast of St John – and pickled outer husk and all. John Gerard, the sixteenth-century herbalist, said that 'the green and tender Nuts boyled in Sugar eaten as a Suckad, are a most pleasant and delectable meat, comfort the stomacke, and expell poison'. Pickled green walnuts are equally alluring, with spices, sugar and vinegar. The unripe nuts can also be made into marmalade as well as a liqueur. Here's how to candy them. Be sure to wear gloves to prevent your hands from being stained black for weeks.

Candied Green Walnuts

Gather walnuts whiles they are small tender and greene with their rinde and all, and make many small holes

Raphaelle Peale, *Still-life: Strawberries, Nuts, &c.*, 1822.

Joseph Decker, *Still-life with Tin Cans and Nuts*, c. 1886.

therein, and after laye them to steepe in water eleven or twelve dayes, more or lesse, cleanse them from the skinne that lyeth on the shelle, without shaling of them, and boyle them in clarified sugar a long time, still putting unto them more and more clarified sugar, because the long boyling will make great waste: in the end put them into vessells with cloves, ginger, and cinnamon, but lesse of the cloves than any of the reste, because they would make them over bitter.[1]

The botanical name of the walnut, *Juglans regia*, denotes regality, and indeed, the nut was associated with Jupiter. *Juglans* basically means Jupiter's acorn, though the Romans called the walnut a Gallic nut. At weddings they would throw walnuts at the happy couple.

In Germanic languages the walnut is a foreigner's nut, *wal* meaning stranger. The most typical walnut is the Persian or English walnut; it seems the latter name was devised to distinguish it from American species. The latter are the black walnut (*J. nigra*) native to North America, *J. californica* and *J. cinerea*, or butternut. The u.s., or rather the Central Valley of California, is the largest exporter of walnuts in the world.

It was long held that to stimulate fresh growth and fruit, the ends of the branches should be beaten with a stick, hence the old saying according to the seventeenth-century poet John Taylor: 'A woman, a spaniel and a walnut tree, / The more they're beaten the better still they be', or in another rhyme with better metre, 'A dog, a wife and a walnut tree: the more you beat them, the better they be'. The deeply pacifist philosopher Bertrand Russell opined about the rhyme:

> I have no experience of the moral effect of flagellation on walnut trees, but no civilized person would now justify the rhyme as regards wives. The reformative effect of punishment is a belief that dies hard, chiefly, I think, because it is so satisfying to our sadistic impulses.[2]

In Aesop's fable, people throw sticks and stones to knock down nuts. It's a short fable: a walnut tree standing by the roadside

The black walnut, native to North America, whole and a cross-section of the shell.

Hans Holbein's *Charitas*, 1543, showing the patient, suffering walnut tree who allows himself to be beaten and shares his nuts.

bore an abundant crop of fruit. To obtain its nuts, passers-by broke its branches with stones and sticks. The walnut tree piteously exclaimed, 'O wretched me! that those whom I cheer with my fruit should repay me with these painful requitals!'

Nutcrackers are designed specifically for walnuts, and many may break their jaws trying to crack open Brazil or macadamia nuts. Even a classic utilitarian nutcracker has a very hard time with these. If you don't have a nutcracker, try this old way of cracking walnuts: hold two walnuts in one hand and squeeze as hard as you can. One will crack the other. Use two hands if necessary.

Beechnut

American readers may think that some candy must be made of beechnuts, since there is a candy company by that name, or at least a brand that still survives and is familiar to Americans as a gum and tobacco company, oh and baby food too: the Beech-Nut Nutrition Corporation. This seems very odd, since the tiny nuts are slightly toxic due to bitter glycosides, which is probably why there has never been commercial production of them. The origin of the name of the company is a mystery.

The beechnut is three-sided with sharp edges, sort of like a pyramid with a rounded base, and it looks as though it is wearing a shaggy coat before the seeds drop out of the husk. The scientific name of the genus of tree that bears the beechnut, *Fagus*, has a truly unbelievable etymology. It is related to *bukenbaum* in Dutch, *buehbaum* and *buche* in German, the same

Floris Claesz. van Dyck, *Still-life*, 1613, showing what appear to be chestnuts, walnuts, acorns and a beechnut.

word as 'book' in English, deriving from the Anglo-Saxon *boece*. Apparently people wrote on beechbark – which never heals over – before they started writing on paper; perhaps they peeled off the bark and wrote on it, and folded it up like a book. However, the word goes even further back – the Proto-Indo-European root *bhagos*, meaning beech tree, is also an ancestor of the Latin *fagus*.

In any case, practically no one eats beechnuts anymore, except for squirrels and intrepid gatherers who manage to find sweet ones.

6

The Modern Industry

Did you know that almonds grown in California must be pasteurized, by either heat or fumigation with propylene oxide, which is used to make polyurethane and is listed by the Environmental Protection Agency as a probable carcinogen? This is no trivial matter: 80 per cent of almonds grown in the world come from California. It was decided in 2007, after several outbreaks of salmonella from raw almonds, that the risk was too great and it would be safest to cook or fumigate them. This had raw-food advocates up in arms. More importantly, one wonders, how does salmonella get on an almond in the first place? It comes from animal faeces, but how do these get on an almond?

I have an idea about how this happened. At about the time when this whole controversy sprung up, I was invited to visit an almond orchard with some students. It was harvest time and the trees were heavy with nuts. In spring the landscape is absolutely blanketed by pinkish white flowers, but by autumn everything is dry and dusty. I should point out that the invitation came from the Almond Board of California, the very people who recommended pasteurization to the United States Department of Agriculture (USDA). So I was hoping to get the dirt on this, and as it turned out I did, literally.

Modern almond harvesting uses a machines that shakes the nuts off the trees.

You might think almonds are picked off trees. At one time they were, mostly by migrant labourers. The trees are fairly short, so maybe it took a little poking to dislodge the nuts, plus a little sorting to remove the tough outer husk. This is nothing like the process today. A little truck is attached to each tree with a belt. It then shakes and rattles, so violently that you would think an earthquake had hit. The shaking brings down everything, even the leaves. Then another machine comes and blows this into neat windrows. Then another sucks everything up – almonds, twigs, rocks and soil – and dumps it into a truck. As you can imagine, it takes several other huge machines, each the size of a house, to get all that soil and debris off. Then other machines remove the husks, take off the shells, and so on. This grower said that it costs several hundred thousand dollars a year in electricity just to run this equipment.

I guess a little soil makes it through the whole process anyway, because that's where the salmonella comes from. It might be from a passing bird, nearby cattle or a mouse; it might be from water, or anywhere else an animal might have had contact. It's the same for the peppers, peanuts and dozens of other plants from which people have been getting salmonella lately. In a nutshell: it's not the plants themselves, but the processing that introduces it. The almonds wouldn't have soil on them if they were picked by hand.

I had an equally profound revelation while visiting the Diamond Walnut factory, just a few miles from my home in downtown Stockton, California. This is no ordinary processing facility. It takes up what seem like a few dozen football fields. I was told that a fifth of all walnuts on Earth pass through its doors. Then there was the noise. It was so unfathomably deafening that we had to wear sound-blocking headsets, and our

Machinery used to dehull walnuts.

guide communicated to the class via a wireless transmitter. To get a sense of the space you need to picture one of the dark, hellish scenes dreamed up by Hieronymus Bosch. He would have felt perfectly at home here, except that in place of monsters dealing exquisite tortures, there were machines clanging, spewing, churning and even shooting laser beams. This is the latest technology for removing the stray bits of shell. As we walked over what seemed acres of makeshift metal ladders, slick with decades of oil droplets, I fully expected someone to slip into the vat like Augustus Gloop, or a hapless character from Upton Sinclair.

Despite all this technological rigmarole, the one thing that stayed firmly in my mind after so many years was a little table set among the demoniacal clatter, where a dozen patient Mexican women, replete with hairnets, sat carefully shelling walnuts by hand. I asked what they were doing there. Apparently the human touch is required to obtain absolutely flawless nuts for export. Chalk up another one for modern technology.

Recipes

Needless to say, modern cooking in general does not make enough use of nuts. They are used in sweets, but how many savoury dishes feature nuts in a starring role? I don't mean their use as a garnish here or there, such as the slivers of almonds on a string-bean casserole or a few walnuts in a loaf of bread. Nor of course do I mean the nut loaves we might associate with the experiments of John Harvey Kellogg over a century ago, or with the hippie generation more recently. It seems that with so much attention being paid to nuts in the current natural food movement, something beyond nut butters and nut milks is needed. On the other hand, most of the world has never lost its deep appreciation for nuts – especially the Middle East and India, where ground nuts are the basis of countless sauces. In Asia coconuts play much the same role. These recipes will hopefully get you thinking in creative ways about using humble nuts in the kitchen.

Cardinals on Horseback

These are a variation on the familiar angels or devils on horseback, here called cardinals because they're reddish from the Campari.

pine nuts
pitted dried apricots
dried black figs

mostarda di fruta
Campari
lardo or prosciutto
escarole leaf, to serve

Soak the apricots and figs in the campari until they are soft and red. Crush the pine nuts a little and mix with some mostarda to keep them together, then stuff the mixture into the dried fruits. Wrap each fruit in a small piece of the lardo and skewer one of each fruit together, to keep the lardo in place. Broil quickly so that the lardo just begins to brown. Serve at once as an appetizer on a leaf of escarole.

Extravagant Couscous

1 box (285 g/10 oz) instant couscous
2 tablespoons clarified butter
pinch of saffron
1 8-oz can (200 ml) chicken broth
1 cup (120 g) pine nuts
1 cup (175 g) zante currants
1 tablespoon capers
handful of finely chopped fresh parsley
pinch of za'atar, to serve

In a skillet fry the couscous in the butter until golden. At the same time heat the chicken broth with the pinch of saffron until bright yellow. Pour the broth into the couscous and stand back to avoid the steam. Quickly add the other ingredients, cover and turn off the heat. Add more boiling water if the mixture looks dry. Leave to stand for about 10 minutes. Serve with a pinch of za'atar on top.

Vegetarian Stuffed Cabbage

1 large head of cabbage
2 cups (230 g) coarsely ground walnuts
½ teaspoon thyme
pinch of ground cumin
1 tablespoon tomato paste
1 chopped onion
1 tablespoon paprika
1 teaspoon salt
2 tablespoons olive oil
sour cream or pistachio cream, to serve

Remove the core of the cabbage with a sharp knife, then boil the entire head of cabbage for 10 minutes. Remove, drain and let cool. Crush the walnuts in a mortar or food processor and add the other ingredients. Continue crushing until incorporated. Remove the whole leaves of cabbage and place a heaped spoonful of the nut mixture in the centre of each leaf. Fold over the thick bottom part of a leaf, then each side, and roll away from you towards the thinnest side to create a tight roll. Repeat with the rest of the cabbage leaves. Line a casserole dish with the rolls, drizzle with a little more olive oil, cover and bake in an oven preheated to 350°F for one hour. Serve with a dollop of sour cream. For a vegan version substitute pistachio cream for the sour cream.

Sun-dried Tomato Quick Cashew Cheese

1 cup (140 g) raw cashews (soaked in water for 2–4 hours and drained)
1 cup (150 g) cherry tomatoes
½ cup (120 g) sundried tomatoes
2 tablespoons lemon juice
¼ teaspoon Himalayan sea salt
¼ teaspoon pepper
¼ teaspoon za'atar or oregano

Place all the ingredients in a food processor and mix them thoroughly. The final texture should not be completely smooth. Serve with Spinach Cracker Bread (below).

Spinach Cracker Bread

1 cup (38 g) spinach
½ cup carrots
1 apple
1 cup (115 g) raw walnuts (soaked in water for 2–4 hours and drained)
½ cup (110 ml) extra-virgin olive oil
¼ teaspoon Himalayan sea salt
¼ teaspoon pepper
¼ teaspoon cumin
¾ cup (100 g) ground golden flaxseed

Finely chop the spinach and carrots in a food processor, and put aside. Finely chop the apple and walnuts and mix into the spinach and carrots. Alternatively, use the leftover pulp after juicing an entire bunch of spinach, 5–6 carrots and 1 apple, then add the finely chopped walnuts to the juicer pulp. Stir in the olive oil and seasoning, then the ground flaxseed. Spread out the mixture onto a dehydrator sheet and dehydrate overnight at 105°F (40°C).

Pine Nut Soup

2 cups (280 g) pine nuts
2 cups (450 ml) water
pinch of salt
pomegranate seeds, sprinkling of cumin or dash of rosewater, to garnish

Place the pine nuts in a blender with the water and salt. Blend and chill. If you like, serve garnished with pomegranate seeds, a sprinkling of cumin or a dash of rosewater.

Acorn Crêpes

1 cup (120 g) acorn flour
1 egg
milk
1 teaspoon unrefined sugar
vanilla extract to taste
¼ teaspoon baking powder
a knob of butter
fillings of your choice

Mix the acorn flour with the egg and enough milk to make a smooth, thin batter. Add the sugar, a few drops of vanilla extract and the baking powder. Let the batter sit for at least an hour. Then heat a large, non-stick pan, drop in the butter and wait until it melts and is sizzling. Pour in enough batter to very thinly cover the surface of the pan, swirling it around until even. You may need to thin the batter with a little water or milk, so that it pours evenly. Remove the crêpe to a plate and continue to make more crêpes until all the batter is used up. Then put something on each crêpe, such as chopped fruit, raspberry or fig jam, or even Nutella (which is a double-nut whammy) and roll it up. You could even use a combination of sweetened cottage and cream cheese. Sprinkle the crêpes with powdered sugar for serving.

Spicy Pili-encrusted Crab Cakes

1 8-oz (225-g) tin of fresh crab meat
1 cup (115 g) finely crushed raw pili nuts
1 cup (125 g) dry breadcrumbs
1 tablespoon mayonnaise

¼ cup (30 g) finely diced green and red bell peppers
1 jalapeno chilli pepper
1 shallot, minced
1 tablespoon fish sauce (patis)
juice of ½ lime
handful coriander (cilantro) leaves
olive oil, for frying
Filipino banana ketchup, to serve

In a large bowl, combine the crab meat with half the crushed nuts and half the breadcrumbs plus all the other ingredients. Mix together the remaining breadcrumbs and crushed nuts and set aside. Form four large cakes with the crab mixture and dredge in the breadcrumb and nut mixture to coat thoroughly on all sides. Fry the cakes gently in olive oil on a medium heat until browned. Serve hot with the banana ketchup on the side.

Chicken Nut Stew

While you often see peanuts in a stewed chicken dish in West Africa, other nuts make an intriguing alternative. Use pistachios or almonds here, or a nut-butter mixture. Regular palm or coconut oil, while not exactly the same as the red palm oil used in Africa, which is more of a condiment than a cooking oil, contributes immeasurably to the flavour and can be found in health-food stores. I would argue that cooking this in a clay pot also adds to the flavour.

1 lb (450 g) chicken thighs with bone and skin
salt and pepper
2 tablespoons palm or coconut oil
3 large tomatoes, skinned and diced
1 onion, diced and sautéed gently until golden brown and soft
1 knob ginger, peeled and grated
3 small red chilli peppers, very finely chopped
3 tablespoons almond or pistachio butter
rice, to serve

Generously season the chicken thighs with salt and pepper, and brown them in a pot in the oil. Add the tomatoes and cooked onion, and water to cover. Add the ginger and chilli peppers to taste. Simmer gently for about an hour. Add the nut butter and stir until thickened. Serve with rice and eat with your fingers if you like.

Smoked Cured Pork Chops with Apples and Pecans

4 thick shoulder pork chops or country ribs
1 tablespoon salt
⅛ teaspoon pink curing salt or Instacure no. 1
1 teaspoon coriander seeds
1 teaspoon whole black peppercorns
1 tablespoon brown sugar
2 tart apples, such as Granny Smiths, cored and cut into wedges,
with peel left on
1 cup (115 g) pecans
3 tablespoons butter
dash of applejack whiskey or calvados
polenta, to serve
kale or broccoli rabe, to serve

Place the pork chops in a large, sturdy plastic bag. Add salts, spices and sugar to cover well. Seal tightly and place in the refrigerator for one week, turning the ingredients every day. Then take the ribs, brush off the whole spices and smoke on an extremely low heat over soaked hickory or applewood chips for about 2 hours. This can be done in a smoker or over coals in a barbecue pit and is technically hot smoking, so the meat will cook through. If you don't have a smoker, it can also be done in a gas grill, with the lid open and the chips placed in a foil packet, but it will take much less time, about 45 minutes or so. Before serving, brown the apples and pecans in the butter, adding the applejack whiskey at the end, and serve over the chops, one per person. Serve with polenta and sautéed bitter greens such as kale or broccoli rabe.

Rupert of Nola's Blancmange
—from *Libro de guisados* (Barcelona, 1525)

Menjar blanch you make in this manner: first take a chicken and 8 ounces of rice flour and half a pound of rosewater [225 ml] and a pound of fine sugar and eight pounds of goat's milk and if you don't have, you take three pounds of white almonds. Then take the chicken which is large and fat and when you wish to make menjar blanch, kill the chicken and pluck it dry and wash it well and put it to boil in a pot in which no thing has ever been cooked. And when the chicken is more than half cooked, take the breasts of the chicken and shred them like saffron strands. And after take the rose water and strew it repeatedly over the strands of chicken. After put all this in a pot, but not of copper, nor recently tinned, or it will pickup the flavor of the tin. And if it has been recently tinned, let it boil with a lot of bread and stew it very well, and thus the flavor of the tin will be removed. Then place in the chicken and take the broth of the same chicken and pour it over the chicken. Have a wooden spoon because it won't take on the flavor of wood, and stir it. Then take half of the milk and place it in the pot with the said chicken, and after place in the flour carefully little by little, stirring constantly so it doesn't stick to the pot. Put next eight dines [dineros, the Castilian version explains that this equals 12 maravedis] of sugar in the pot and let it boil, stirring more the whole time so that it never rests, adding little by little the milk until it is all used up, and be careful of it burning. And when the menjar blanch becomes clear, the chicken is good, and be sure not to add in more milk. And when the menjar blanch becomes like a roasted cheese, it's cooked, and place in the rose water and after the grease from the pot, being clean of salt pork. Realize that from a chicken you can make six plates. Remove it from the fire and let it rest and then make plates and place on it fine sugar. And in this way you make menjar blanc perfectly, as is proven every time.

Dukkah and *Charoset*

Here are two great versions of *dukkah* and a Sephardic *charoset*. The former goes really well with torn pita bread dipped in olive oil, the latter with broken pieces of matzoh. The quantities and proportions are entirely up to you.

Toast whole unblanched almonds in a dry skillet until fragrant. Let cool, then crush them into a coarse powder in a wooden mortar, move to a bowl and set aside to cool. Toast cumin seeds, coriander, peppercorns and a small piece of cinnamon stick. Pound them finely or grind in a spice grinder. Add to the almonds. You can substitute hazelnuts for the almonds, or just add some.

To make *charoset*, to the above mixture add some finely chopped dates, raisins and – if you like – apricots. Drizzle in some honey, a little vinegar and red wine. Pound further until it resembles the mortar with which the Hebrew slaves set bricks in Egypt. Serve on matzoh with bitter herbs, or as a little 'Hillel sandwich', charoset between two pieces of matzoh. Nowadays the bitter herb is just freshly grated horseradish and nothing else – so pungent that it goes straight up your nose and into your brain, but combined with the sweet, nutty *charoset*, it is simply remarkable.

Hazelnut Torte

1 cup (100 g) hazelnuts
1 stick (125 g) butter at room temperature
1 cup (125 g) sugar
4 eggs, separated
pinch of cream of tartar
2 tablespoons Frangelico liqueur
½ cup (125 g) Mexican queso fresco
2 tablespoons flour
powdered sugar and cinnamon

Toast the hazelnuts gently in a pan until lightly browned, then crush in a mortar or food processor. In a bowl cream the butter with the sugar until lightly coloured, add the egg yolks one by one, then the liqueur, and mix thoroughly. Add the queso fresco and incorporate thoroughly. Stir in the flour. Next beat the egg whites in a separate clean bowl with a miniscule pinch of cream of tartar until stiff. Gently fold the egg whites into the hazelnut mixture. Transfer to a springform pan lined with greaseproof paper and buttered lightly. Bake for 40 minutes in an oven preheated to 350°F (175°C). Let cool. Put the torte on a plate and dust with powdered sugar and cinnamon.

Mandorla Nog
(for 2 servings)

1 cup (225 ml) fresh almond milk
1 shot (1.5 U.S. fl. oz/45 ml) amaretto liqueur
2 shots (3 U.S. fl. oz/90 ml) brandy
1 raw egg
1 tablespoon pure maple syrup
dash vanilla extract
whole nutmeg

Prepare the almond milk in advance by placing a cup of raw peeled and blanched almonds in a blender and adding one cup (225 ml) of very hot water. Pulse the blender until the almonds are finely ground. Leave for a few hours or overnight. Strain through a fine sieve. Chill the almond milk thoroughly in the refrigerator. Mix all the ingredients well and chill in the refrigerator before serving. Pour into two glasses and top with a grating of whole nutmeg.

References

1 What is a Nut?

1 R. W. Spjut, 'A Systematic Treatment of Fruit Types',
  Memoires of the New York Botanical Garden, 70 (1994), pp. 1–182,
  at www.worldbotanical.com.
2 Galen of Pergamum, *Properties of Foodstuffs*, trans. Owen
  Powell (Cambridge, 2003), pp. 97–8.
3 Jean Bruyerin-Champier, *De re cibaria* (Lyons, 1560), p. 79.
4 William Coles, *Adam in Eden* (London, 1657).
5 Dioscorides, *De Materia Medica* (Lyons, 1552), p. 134.
6 Galen, *On Food and Diet*, trans. Mark Grant (London, 2000),
  pp. 132–3.

2 Nuts to Chew

1 *An English Translation of the Sushruta Samhita*, ed. Kaviraj Kunja
  Lal Bhishagratna, vol. II (self-published, 1911), pp. 483, 510.
2 Rembert Dodoens, *A New Herball* (London, 1595), p. 855.

3 Nuts in Cooking

1 Jean Bottéro, *The Oldest Cuisine in the World* (Chicago, IL,
  2004), pp. 19–23.

2 *Apicius*, ed. Chris Grocock and Sally Grainger (Totnes, 2003), p. 143.

3 *The Viandier of Taillevent*, trans. Terence Scully (Ottowa, 1988), p. 508. Here I use my own slightly different translation.

4 Martino of Como, *The Art of Cooking*, trans. Jeremy Parzen (Berkeley, CA, 2005), p. 83.

5 Ortensio Lando, *Commentario delle più notabili et mostruose cose d'Italia* (Venice, 1553), p. 65, 'Pillade de Luca: fu il primo che mangiasse castagnazzi, & minestra di semola, & di questo riportò loda'.

6 Leonhart Fuchs, *De historia stirpium* (Lyons, 1555), p. 446.

7 Friederich Fluckiger, *Pharmacographia* (London, 1879), p. 245; Alfred Franklin, *La vie privée d'autrefois*, vol. III (Paris, 1889), pp. 44–6.

8 *Libellus de Arte Coquinaria*, ed. Rudolph Grewe and Constance B. Hieatt (Tempe, AZ, 2001). The translation here is mine, and intentionally literal.

9 *Cuyre on Inglysch*, ed. Constance B. Hieatt and Sharon Butler (London, 1985).

10 *Libre de Sent Soví*, ed. Rudolph Grewe (Barcelona, 1979), p. 141.

11 *Libro di cucina del scolo XIV* (Anonimo Veneziano), ed. Ludovico Frati (Bologna, 1986), p. 13.

12 ub Gent Hs. 1035, c.a. Serrure, ed., *Keukenboek uitgegeven naar een Handschrift der vijftiende eeuw* (Ghent, 1872). The Dutch text can be found at www.coquinaria.nl with a translation by Christiane Muusers, which is somewhat different from mine.

4 Nuts Familiar and Exotic

1 See 'Mrs Roner's Answers to Questions', *Ladies Home Journal*, xv (July 1898), p. 32.

2 Bartolomeo Stefani, *L'Arte di ben cucinare* (Mantova, 1662), p. 64.

3 Antonius Gazius, *Corona florida medicinae* (Venice, 1491), pp. mvi verso; fol Cix v, 1514 edn.

4 Journal of Heredity (American Genetic Association), v
(1914), p. 179.

5 Nuts in Sweets, Snacks and Junk Food

1 Charles Etienne and Jean Liebault, Maison Rustique or The
Countrie Farme, trans. Richard Surflet (London, 1616), p. 421.
2 Bertrand Russell, Unpopular Essays (London, 1950), p. 148.

Select Bibliography

Every nut covered in this volume deserves a whole book. Until those are written, here are some suggestions for further reading:

Allen, Zel, *The Nut Gourmet* (Summertown, TN, 2006)
Hill, Lewis and Leonard Perry, *The Fruit Gardener's Bible: A Complete Guide to Growing Fruits and Nuts in the Home Garden* (North Adams, MA, 2011)
Duke, James A., *Handbook of Nuts* (New York, 1989)
Freinkel, Susan, *American Chestnut* (Berkeley, CA, 2007)
Loomis, Susan Hermann, *Nuts in the Kitchen: More than 100 Recipes for Every Taste and Occasion* (New York, 2012)
Lowenfeld, Claire, *Britain's Wild Larder: Nuts* (London, 1957)
Menninger, Edwin A., *Edible Nuts of the World* (Stuart, FL, 1977)
Rosengarten Jr, Frederic, *The Book of Edible Nuts* (Mineola, NY, 1984)

Websites and Associations

Almond Board of California
www.almondboard.com

Australia Macadamia Society
www.macadamias.org

The Brazil Nut Industry: Past, Present and Future
www.nybg.org/bsci/braznut

California Pistachio Commission
www.pistachios.org

California Walnut Board
www.walnuts.com

Cashews, The George Mateljan Foundation
www.whfoods.com

Coconut Research Center
www.coconutresearchcenter.org

Hazelnut Growers of Oregon
www.hazelnutgrowersoforegon.com

Mauna Loa Macadamia Nuts
www.maunaloa.com

National Pecan Sellers Association
www.ilovepecans.org/nutrition.html

Pili Nuts
www.pilinuts.org

The Pros and Cons of Kola Nuts
www.ghanaweb.com

Photo Acknowledgements

The author and the publishers wish to express their thanks to the below sources of illustrative material and /or permission to reproduce it.

Ken Albala: pp. 16, 19, 27, 28, 31, 43, 49, 57, 72, 75, 78, 80, 85, 86, 92, 95; The Art Institute of Chicago: p. 93 (Gift of Jamee J. and Marshall Field 1991.100); © The Trustees of the British Museum, London: p. 56; Jim McDougall: p. 83; Flusel: p. 66; iStockphoto: pp. 13 (Veronika Rossimaa), 26 (narvikk), 44 (tunart), 100 (David Gomez Photography), 101 (Carmen Reed); Library of Congress, Washington, DC: pp. 64, 71; Rolfmueller: p. 36; Shutterstock: pp. 6 (Markus Mainka), 14 (Sue Robinson), 21 (Mukesh Kumar), 23 (paul prescott), 34 (wasanajai), 45 (magouillat photo), 73 (Danny E. Hooks), 74 (Kozlenko), 76 (AtthameeNi), 90 (Hayati Kayhan); Stock.xchng: p. 17 (Bill Hardwick), 38 (Mirabelle Pictures), 39 (TJUKTJUK), 42 (graletta); Victoria & Albert Museum, London: pp. 35, 52, 69; Image © Yale University Art Gallery: p. 94.

Index

italic numbers refer to illustrations; **bold** to recipes